SUCCESS:

FULL RELATING

Spirituality for the 21st Century and Beyond

by

Friar Justin Belitz, O.F.M.

Published by

Bloomington, Indiana
(812) 837-9226
info@PenandPublish.com
www.PenandPublish.com

Front cover heart-rose artwork
painted by and courtesy of Charleyn Moore

Cover photograph courtesy of Garry Chilluffo
www.Chilluffo.com

ISBN: 978-0-9817264-4-1

LCCN: 2010923427

This book is printed on acid free paper.

Printed in the USA

**This book is dedicated to
the many people who have helped me,
and continue to help me, on my journey
of personal growth and development!**

ACKNOWLEDGEMENTS

The insights contained in this volume have taken a lifetime to surface. It is impossible to list all of the many people who have helped me along the way. Both my immediate and extended families began that process the day I was born. The parish community at Immaculate Conception Church in Omaha, Nebraska, especially the Franciscan Sisters who taught me in grade school, continued my relational education.

The Franciscan Friars of the Sacred Heart Province, as well as friars from around the world, have been, and continue to be, my support in struggling to live the ideals of Francis of Assisi – and to model them for others. The Hermitage staff and volunteers, for the past quarter of a century, have always been there for me, especially during the challenging times and when I was the difficult and demanding "fly in the ointment"! The Priest Support Group and the Meditation Support Group to which I belong continue to help keep me on track. My students from around the world; benefactors who have supported my teaching and preaching globally; as well as casual acquaintances, brief encounters with those who serve me in restaurants, the supermarket, department stores – all have been my teachers, and I am forever grateful for their presence in my life, in my work, and in my personal growth and development.

Realizing all reality is one and that love is the power that holds us all together, I strive to send the Divine Energy of Love to all of these individuals daily. May we together create peace in our own hearts and then in our world!

Table of Contents

Foreword

Today's challenging problems are merely symptoms of a dualistic way of thinking that continues to create disharmony on the Earth. What is needed, now more than ever, is a new way of relating to one another. Einstein said, "We cannot solve our problems with the same thinking we used when we created them." Fr. Justin Belitz has provided us with a powerful yet simple guidebook for a better way of living and loving on the journey. He challenges us to see through the eyes of love and then to put that love into action. In a world dominated by fear, the only answer will be the transforming power of love.

As a radio host, I've had the privilege of interviewing the top social change agents and spiritual teachers in the country. What I find exceptional about Fr. Justin Belitz is the way he can take deep spiritual and psychological insights and communicate them in everyday language. He is a refreshing voice that calls people to a higher way of thinking and being in the world. Justin understands that personal transformation always precedes social transformation. We need to learn how to become peaceful within while taking compassionate action. We must *be* it in order to *see* it.

Success:Full Relating will assist you in being fully engaged in life and with those who matter most to you. It will challenge old paradigms of thinking and encourage you to *see* people and situations through new eyes. This beautifully written book will also inspire your heart toward selfless service in the world. The time is now for a new spirituality for the 21st century. Together, we can usher in a new humanity that will better serve us all. With this book, Fr. Justin Belitz continues to be a leading voice in this revolution of love that ignites and unites our beloved community.

> Richard Brendan
> Founder & Spiritual Director
> JourneysFire Productions
> Indianapolis, Indiana

Preface

Many years ago I read that writing helps to clarify a person's ideas. With this belief in mind, I am writing primarily to clarify my thoughts on relationships. I am not interested in proving anything or trying to gain "followers."

Of course, I want to share my ideas. At the core of my being, I am a teacher, who has a need to share truth and wisdom with anyone who cares to listen. My hope is that as I write, I can understand relationships better and so improve the quality of my life. Perhaps my sharing will help you to deal more effectively with relationships in your life.

It is not difficult to understand the seven principles I have gathered in this book. The challenge is to apply them in real-life situations. For your consideration, after each chapter, I have included exercises I use daily, and which are important in my workshops. They may be useful in helping you to put these simple principles into practice in your daily life.

The stories I use to illustrate the principles of this book are sometimes altered to protect the identity of individuals involved. Sometime the stories are fictional to illustrate the application of a principle. Sometimes they are real, with the true names of the persons involved.

I hope you will enjoy the experience of this book, but more important, I hope you will find ideas and tools that will make your life richer and more enjoyable!

SUCCESS: FULL RELATING

Responsible Spirituality

For a lifetime, I have carefully gathered and chosen ideals, values, priorities, and principles from my personal life experience. The total sum of these finds I refer to as my "life package." When I am reading a book or listening to a lecture, I am always open to new ideas, but I pick and choose only those that fit into *my* "life package." If I come across an idea that gives me insight into some part of my life, I insert that idea into its proper place in my "life package." However, if I find a thought that does not fit into my "life package," I simply put it aside and move on.

I believe that you, the reader, come to the experience of this book in much the same way. You will read this material through the background of *your* "life package" (your ideals, values, priorities, principles and life experience) which you have carefully chosen over *your* lifetime. My suggestion is that you examine the ideas of this book, take whatever fits into your "life package," and leave the rest.

A second point I want to make is that I write these pages as a friend exposing some personal insights, not as an expert who has the "truth." I happen to be a Franciscan friar and a Roman Catholic priest, but what I write is not theology. What I am sharing is my personal spirituality.

Theology is a very precise science, but it has some major, built-in challenges. For example, theology deals with the spirit world, which is infinite. How, then, can theologians *adequately* express anything in the spirit world, when human language is finite? The answer to this question is simple: They can't! One thing theologians do is coin words. But this can cause difficulty, since one tradition uses one set of words, and another tradition uses another. Christian theologians, for example, define Ultimate Reality in terms of "God" and/or "the Trinity." Buddhists, on the other hand, define ultimate reality in terms of "no thing." Jewish rabbis base their description of ultimate reality on Old Testament symbols like "a Pillar of Fire" or "a Voice in the Sky." Of course, none of these expressions adequately convey the *full* meaning of "Ultimate Reality" - a fact with which all theologians agree.

The challenge, as I see it, is this: Each religion has *preferred* expressions which they consider to be "right" (but none of which are adequate). In this kind of mindset, expressions other than those that are preferred are considered to be "wrong" or "heretical." In the past, there have been arguments, fights, and even wars over which expression is "right." In this sense, theology can be challenging and divisive.

In spirituality, however, personal experience is the measuring stick and can be different for each person. Spirituality, then, is more unifying in its effect and more flexible in its expressions of the spirit world. For example, I can share with you how I relate to myself, to others, to things, to life experience, to God, etc., but I cannot impose my mode of relating on another person because each of us relates in a different way. In spirituality, there is no "right" or "wrong." In spirituality there is only the question "Is this *appropriate* for me or not?" What works for one person may not be appropriate for another person. Spirituality is very personal and changes with every person. In spirituality there is infinite diversity.

As a Franciscan, for example, I promise to live a simple life with few things. As a result I have only one suit, one religious habit, enough underwear for a week, etc. This approach is appropriate for me. For the average family, however, this approach may not be appropriate. Parents who have a duty to provide for the necessities of their children may have a need for more clothing. A businessman may have a need for a larger wardrobe. Adult children caring for elderly parents have still other needs. Each of these cases is unique and, therefore, we cannot say one situation is "good" and the others are "bad." We simply accept each situation as different and know that each case must be handled differently.

In Western mysticism, we have many different schools of spirituality – for example, Franciscan, Dominican, Augustinian, Jesuit, and many others. The Franciscan Order was created by St. Francis, who was Italian. He had a passion to know about the loving process, and therefore his spirituality is said to be all "heart."

The Jesuits, on the other hand, were founded by St. Ignatius, who used the idea of an "army" as his model for relating. In his approach, obedience and knowledge are very important, and, as you may know, the Jesuits are dedicated to and known for their work in education. Their spirituality is said to be all "head."

These descriptions are, of course, generalizations, but they do point out different ways individuals can relate. These differences do not mean that the Franciscan approach is better than the Jesuit approach. They simply mean that people who are more into "heart" will fit better into Franciscan spirituality and those who are more "head" will fit better into Jesuit spirituality. The irony is that this diversity is what makes the Catholic Church so rich. "Catholic" means "universal." Therefore, in terms of spirituality, there is a place for everyone!

As a result of the above considerations, I want to state again that my purpose is to share personal insights. I am not on a campaign trail! I will speak from my *own* experience but with the understanding that *some* of these experiences *may* be similar to yours and may help to give you insight into your own experience. Other of these experiences may not relate to you at all. However, if your reading helps you better understand how you relate, you will be in a position to give appropriate direction to your life and to experience the fullness to which, I believe, we all have a right!

Spirituality

A. Definition

At the outset, I want to clarify a few important ideas. First of all, let me say a little about spirituality. For me (and, I think, for a good many other people), the meaning of "spirituality" is at least fuzzy, if not downright confusing. I have personally examined several definitions but always put them in the context of my experience. After many years, I have found this definition to be useful and practical for me: *Spirituality is the way you relate.* By that, I mean the way you relate to yourself, the way you relate to others, as well as the way you relate to things, to life experience, to God, and to every other aspect of life.

If you accept this definition, you may be able to understand that everyone already has a spirituality. For example, when I get up in the morning, the first thing I do is to look at the clock (since I never use an alarm). I have a good relationship with clocks. They help me organize my life, but they do not rule my life! Clocks help me to be efficient, help me to organize my day, and help me to get more satisfying experiences from my life.

Next, I get out of bed and move to the floor and do push-ups. Exercise is an important part of my life, and as I exercise, I pay attention to how I am performing, how I feel, and I remind myself that exercise helps me stay healthy.

My next task is a set of jumping exercises during which I repeat a set of positive affirmations that relate to seven areas of my life. Jumping helps to remove toxins from my body and promotes health. The affirmations provide mind exercise for mental health. My relationship with mental exercise is something that I have carefully developed over the years and which has enriched my life tremendously.

Having completed the jumping exercises, I do a 15-minute meditation. This experience relates to my faith life. Meditation is prayer, and something that is essential for balance in my life. Meditation helps me relax physically and mentally, but it also brings me to conscious awareness of the God Presence that is with me all the time. My practice of meditation is an expression of my relationship with God (Universal Intelligence or Cosmic Energy or any other term you may wish to use for Ultimate Reality) and helps me develop a healthy spiritual life. Sometimes during meditation I get understanding of a dream, or a solution to a problem in my life, or information about a goal for my future, etc. All of the above experiences create a good relationship for me with sleep, meditation, God, and dreams.

And so it goes throughout the day. Everything that I do expresses a relationship I have with the things I see, the people I meet, the life experience I have, etc. How I relate as I go through the day is simply an expression of my spirituality.

B. The Way You Relate Will Be Consistent in Every Area of Your Life

Because, for me, spirituality is the way I relate, the manner in which I relate will be consistent in every area of my life. For example, if I relate in a negative way to myself, I will relate in a negative way to others. The opposite is also true; if I relate in a positive way to myself, I will be positive when relating to other people. Remember, however, that you, and you alone, make the choice of how you relate.

As a teenager, I had a poor self-image. When I was in college, the dean of students called me into his office for an interview. One of the observations he made was this: "Justin," he said, "you have a very attractive personality." That statement took me by surprise, so much so that I wanted to turn around to see if he were talking to someone else! He then explained that when he first saw me, it was in the recreation room. The room was crowded, but he noticed that several students were engaging me in conversation. He pointed out several other similar situations, and after that interview, I began to pay more attention. For the first time in my life, I realized that I did indeed attract others by my personality. This bit of information allowed me to see myself in a more positive light, and I began to feel better about myself. At the same time, I began to see the dean (and others in authority) in a more positive light. I even began to see the positive side of fellow students whom I didn't like! It was as if I had been living in a darkened room, and when I moved into another space where it was brighter, I was able to see everyone and everything in a different way!

This process works the same way for you, or anyone else who may have a poor self-image. I once knew a gentleman who had a high office in the Church. However, he saw himself as "pushed aside," psychologically and emotionally "abused," and truly a "victim." It was amazing for me to see how he could "put down" other people, and exert his authority in a rude and abusive way. It was easy for me to see that, because he had a negative self-image, he was negative to others also.

How you relate to yourself will also show up in the way that you relate to things. I know a young man who saw himself as fitting into the universe in the same way that American Indians see themselves fitting into the universe. He realized that there must be a place for everything, and it is good to have everything in its place. As a result, this young man decided to live only with the few things he *needed.*

He chose not to have a car and to use public transportation because of his respect for Mother Earth. He lives a simple lifestyle with few things *and* he is comfortable and happy.

On the other hand, I know a woman who has little control over herself. As a result, she has little control over the physical space in which she lives. At one point in time, she invited me to bless her home. I walked into the messiest space I have ever seen! I couldn't get through the kitchen without walking on clothing, bags, and even trash. Lack of control in her own life showed itself in her lack of control over the material things in her life.

The way you relate will be consistent in every other area of your life. For that reason, it is valuable to know exactly how you relate!

C. Discover Your Spirituality

Given the above, you may now realize that spirituality is not something you have to learn. It is already in place in your life. Your task is to discover what your spirituality is!

Every day, throughout the day, you are using patterns of relating that you have created over your entire lifetime. You already have an idea of who you are, and so you relate to that perceived reality in the same way, every day, all day. Let me use an example.

Suppose every morning you see yourself in the mirror as a good-looking, talented person. You think about the success you already have in your life, and you know that you can create an even better future. You look ahead into the coming day, eager for new and exciting experiences. You enjoy improving your life and making the world a better place. In short, you relate to yourself, to others, to things, and to life experience in a positive way.

On the other hand, you can relate to yourself in a completely different way. Suppose you wake up in the morning and see yourself in the mirror as someone "average." You think to yourself, "Why can't I be more productive at work?" You ask yourself, "Why can't I be as important in the family as my brother?" With this kind of thought process, you walk into a new day feeling inadequate, even depressed. Relating in this way to yourself, to others, to things, and to life experience will create a completely different kind of life experience.

To discover what your spirituality is, ask yourself questions like these: "Am I happy being the person I am? Do I know what my talents are? Do I know what my weaknesses are? Do I accept myself as I am?"

You can also ask yourself questions that relate to others: "Do I see the good in others? Do I talk about the good things that I see in others? Do I see the advantages and opportunities in the relationships I presently have with others? Am I aware of a Divine Presence in others?"

You can examine your relationship with things in the same manner: "What things do I value? Am I in charge of things, or are things in charge of me? Do I have a need to acquire things? Am I satisfied with the things that I *need,* or do I always want more? Can I give things away easily? Can I give with joy without expecting anything in return?"

Questions like these will help you discover how you relate and therefore what your spirituality is.

D. Spirituality Is a Choice

Given the above, perhaps you can better understand that your "spirituality" is already in place. Every day you use patterns of relating to yourself, others, things, God, life experience, etc. You are the one who has created these patterns; therefore, it is you, and you alone, who can change these patterns. Might I suggest that as we go through this volume and you clarify how you presently relate, that you ask yourself, "Is this the way I *want* to relate in the future?"

The way you have related in the past has created the life experience you have today. Remember, spirituality has nothing to do with "right" or "wrong," but rather with what is "appropriate" or "inappropriate." My point is this: If you choose to relate in ways that are appropriate for you, you will create a satisfying life experience, but if you choose ways of relating that are not appropriate for you, you will create a dissatisfying life experience. The Scriptures say, "By their fruits you will know them." If your life is satisfying, then you know that you are making appropriate choices, but if your life is dissatisfying, then you know that you are making inappropriate choices. Remember, however, that what is appropriate for one person may not be appropriate for another person. Spirituality is a very personal thing and changes with every individual. Responsible choices are the key to success in every area of life.

As my brothers and I were growing up, my parents were insistent that we show respect to everyone, especially those in the family. We were taught to use the words "please," "thank you," "may I," etc. This approach was reinforced by the nuns who were our teachers in school. We chose to put these directives into practice, and our lives were "full." We had lots of friends, teachers respected us, neighbors valued us, and we felt love from everyone.

However, there were some youngsters in the neighborhood who refused to accept these simple life directives. One of my classmates (Richard, I think, was his name) used foul language and bullied students, even teachers! He was disliked by everyone and must have been very unhappy. One day he was trying to prove how "strong" he was. As we began to cross over a bridge on the way home, someone dared Richard to jump off the bridge. He did, and broke his leg! In my estimation, Richard had little, if any, respect for himself, and therefore, little or no respect for others. Because of this poor relationship with himself and with others, he did not create a very satisfying life for himself.

E. Two Categories of Spirituality

In order to simplify as much as possible, I want to consider two basic categories of spirituality. The first is the Matriarchal (or Creation) Model and the second is the Patriarchal (or the Fall/Redemption) Model. These categories are mental constructs that have helped me understand relationships in my life and how I deal with them. I hope they will help you in the same way.

1. The Matriarchal (Creation) Model

The Matriarchal Model (also referred to as the Creation or Servant Model) is the one that Jesus gave us. It is an approach in which people are considered to be on an equal footing. This comparison is built on the ideal relationship of a mother and her child. In this model, the mother is seen as having an "equal" relationship with the child. The mother sees herself as a servant whose job is to care for the child. She does not see this position as demeaning. The relationship can truly be referred to as "servant leadership." The mother feels fulfilled as she serves the child. She feeds, bathes, cleans, protects, educates, and loves the child. All this gives her great happiness and fulfillment. Her intention is not to have "power over" the child but rather to have "power with" the child.

This is the unifying model that Jesus gave us and which we refer to as "servant leadership." Jesus was constantly trying to help us understand this model as one that unifies. He said, "I am in my Father and you are in me and I in you." He prayed that this unity would be a reality, "that they may all be one, as you, Father, are in me and I in you, that they may be one in us. . . ."

If we were to diagram this model, we could use an image like this:

In this diagram, God (the Trinity) is the triangle, and humanity is the stick figure. This model depicts God as being one with all human beings. This kind of relationship between God and humans, indeed with all creation, was considered radical at the time of Jesus (even today this idea is considered by many to be radical!). If we are all one with God, then we must say that all human beings are intrinsically good. This approach to spirituality begins with "Original Blessing" – God blessing the universe, so that everything in it is considered to be good (see the Book of Genesis).

If you accept this approach to relationships, then it follows that all human beings are one with God – that we are all connected – that we share one Life Source in which we are bound into a unifying whole!

As one, we are able to experience exciting and revitalizing pleasure, able to celebrate shared power with the universe, able to rejoice in change that leads to a better reality, able to live in trusting relationships, and even able to experience ecstasy in unconditional love!

All of the above can be outlined in this following list of characteristics that describe the Matriarchal Model:

Matriarchal (Creation) Model
Power With
Original Blessing
Unity
Sharing
Movement
Ecstasy and Trust
Change
Cosmic Awareness
Pleasure
Universal
Dialog
Love of Life

This approach to relationships was very threatening to the patriarchy of Jewish and Roman leaders at the time of Jesus. Unconditional love for everyone, and totally equal relationships everywhere, would completely destroy the power structures of both the secular and religious worlds of that time.

Over the past 2,000 years, the ideals of this Matriarchal Model have been kept alive by people such as Florence Nightingale, Hildegard of Bingen, Julian of Norwich, Mechthild of Magdeburg, Francis of Assisi, Therese (the Little Flower), and many others. In our own time, Mahatma Gandhi, Mother Teresa, Martin Luther King Jr., the Dalai Lama, Pope John XXIII, and many others believed in and supported the Matriarchal Model.

Let me point out a few things from the life of St. Francis that demonstrate how the Matriarchal Model works in a practical situation. St. Francis never intended to start an "Order" (which is a patriarchal structure). His idea was to start a "movement" – based on the ideals of the Gospel. However, when his ideals began to attract others in large numbers, Church authorities insisted that he write a "Rule."

In his mind, Francis considered everyone in the community to be his "brother." Everyone was on an equal footing. No one was "over" anyone else; rather all were called to serve one another. Francis did not "push" anyone anywhere, so his "rule" was simply a collection of Scripture quotes that described the lifestyle of Jesus. Eventually, Francis was forced to move his community into the structure of a religious order, but he never lost his ideal of "a Brotherhood."

Toward the end of his life, when the Franciscan Order had grown to thousands, the Brothers began to interpret the Rule in two different ways. Younger friars found the approach of Francis too difficult and wanted an easier lifestyle. Others wanted to keep the original ideal of Francis. Francis, himself, did not side with either group. He simply told the Brothers that he was called to live his particular form of life and that he would continue to live that ideal.

At that point, the Order split into two branches, each interpreting the same Rule as *they* believed it should be lived. Neither group was considered to be "right." Members of each felt they had to live the Rule the way, they believed, God had called them to live it.

Today, our Order has three branches, all following the same Rule but each using a different interpretation. This is the Matriarchal Model in practice: unity in diversity!

Francis respected the individuality of each person as an expression of God's infinite diversity, and that ideal has been carefully guarded and protected over the past 800 years. Individuality for each friar is still an important value in our spirituality.

Francis wanted us to celebrate our uniqueness within the context of one loving community. This is the way he saw Jesus relate, and what today we refer to as Matriarchal or Creation Spirituality.

In my own life, I experienced both the Matriarchal and the Patriarchal Models in my own family. As children, my brothers and I understood that Daddy was the head of the household, Ma was under him, and we were under both of them. Ma understood this structure and was always careful to let Daddy know that he was the head of the family. However, Ma held all the power!

Let me explain. My dad, being the head of the family and the disciplinarian, held the place of power and authority. He was a loving and kind person, and we loved him a great deal, *but* we were afraid of him. This relationship was definitely in the Patriarchal Model. On the other hand, my mom was our friend. We were on an equal level with her. We could talk to her about anything. Her relationship with us was in the Matriarchal Model.

In practice, if we wanted something from Daddy, we didn't go to him; we went to Ma. For example, we could approach her and ask, "Can we have the keys to the car on Saturday night?" If she said "Yes," it was a done deal! She then would approach Daddy, telling him how we had done our work in the yard, in the house, at the family grocery store, and at the gas station. Her approach was; "Don't you think they deserve a night out?" She was careful to let Daddy know that as head of the household, he was making the decisions, but at the same time, Ma always got what she wanted.

Please note that with my dad, the Patriarchal Model was at work. He had the position of authority and "power over" the family. With my Mom, the Matriarchal Model was at work. She was our friend; we had an equal relationship with her, she was a servant because she was the nurturing person in the family, and she carried all the power!

In the Matriarchal Model, Jesus is the perfect lover. Because of his love for everyone, he had enormous power to influence people, but he did not control them! This kind of power is what patriarchy fears – even today. Unconditional love is a "dangerous" teaching for leaders who are in a Patriarchal Model. That is precisely why Jewish and Roman leaders wanted to get rid of Jesus. That is why patriarchy got rid of Martin Luther King Jr., and John and Robert Kennedy.

The following diagram may help you to understand some characteristics of the Creation Model and how they differ from the characteristics of the Patriarchal Model.

MODELS FOR RELATING
(Spirituality)

Matriarchal (Creation)	Patriarchal (Fall/Redemption)
Power With	Power Over
Original Blessing	Original Sin
Unity	Division
Sharing	Greed
Movement	Institution
Ecstasy and Trust	Sin and Guilt
Change	Status Quo
Cosmic Awareness	Selfish Awareness
Pleasure	Pain
Universal	Provincial
Dialog	War
Love of Life	Love of Death

Today, the Matriarchal Model is noticeable in the "Green" movement. For thousands of years, the Christian world quoted the text from Genesis: "Be fruitful and multiply. Fill the earth and subdue it." The interpretation was that human beings were "in charge" and could do what they wanted with the earth. This, of course, is the Patriarchal Model at work.

In the Matriarchal Model the realization is that all of creation is *one*. Our task is not to control the Universe – that is impossible! Our task is to work with the Universe toward love and peace! This is the challenge that Jesus gave us in this Matriarchal (Unitive) Model. Everyone and everything has equal status: women, the poor, widows, the sick, animals, all of nature, and today we would add people of color, gay, lesbian, bisexual and transsexual persons, criminals, drug addicts, etc. It is this spirituality of equality that got Jesus into trouble. This spirituality is still dangerous, in the 21st century!

The Matriarchal Model is a real challenge for the entire planet, but it is not an impossibility! There have been whole societies based on this model. The American Indians, for example, perceived themselves as part of the whole of Creation. They could not imagine the concept of owning land. The land was a free entity in itself, something to be used and cared for, not something to be owned and exploited. When American Indians hunted, it was for food, not for sport. The meat was used for food, the hide for clothing or shelter, the entrails became food for other animals, and even the bones were used for tools and for decoration. There was no waste!

Today, there is a strong movement throughout the world to build equal relationships with all of creation. We are now beginning to see ourselves as *part* of the whole in which we must think about, and care for, everyone and everything in Creation. Equal relationships are essential if we are to survive on the planet as a species.

This morning, I was watching the news on TV. A mother was sitting on the floor in the corner of her empty living room sobbing because of foreclosure on her home. At the auction, another woman (who lived 200 miles away, and who knew the other woman's situation), purchased the building. She then approached the tearful mother and told her that she and her family could continue to live in the house. They worked out a financial arrangement in which the family would rent to buy. Both women left the auction in a state of great joy. The mother and her family because they had their home back and the other woman who purchased the house because she was able to help someone in need and at the same time succeed financially! This is the Matriarchal Model working in our world today!

Social and political change toward the Matriarchal Model began late in the 1800s, when women began to see themselves as equals with men. That movement is still in operation, but since that time the African American community, under the leadership of Dr. Martin Luther King Jr., began its journey toward equality. Now other minorities are seeing themselves as equal to others and slowly, slowly, we are moving toward equality in every segment of the world population.

Even in religious communities, like ours, the Matriarchal Model is working. For many years, the Vatican forced the Franciscan Order to fit into the Patriarchal Model. We were directed to live a monastic life (even though we are not monks), and we were labeled a "clerical order" (i.e., an order of priests), even though it was clear that Francis wanted a "Brotherhood" of equals.

When the Second Vatican Council (1962–1965) convened, it directed all religious communities to go back to the ideals of their founders. At that point, we Franciscans made major changes. Before Vatican II, we identified our members as either Brothers or Fathers. Fathers were friars who had theological degrees and who were ordained to the priesthood. Brothers were not ordained. Built into this system was a hierarchy in which the Fathers were considered to be "better" or "higher" than the Brothers. Since the Council, we now identify everyone in the Order as "Friar" so that no one knows who is a priest and who is not. It is a way of "equalizing" everyone into the Matriarchal Model.

In business, there is the same motion toward the Matriarchal Model and servant leadership. Consider the many companies that are moving into the multilevel structure. In this structure, individuals can enter the business, become their own bosses, and work in an environment where they are supported by others in the company. When one person succeeds, everyone succeeds. Amway was one of the first to use this model. I was asked to give presentations to groups within the Amway company and met wonderful people. One couple wanted a way to be together but at the same time to generate the income that would be necessary to provide education for all their children. Amway provided that opportunity. They worked out of their home, worked together to create a very successful business, and today are able to finance all their own needs as well as those of their children.

2. The Patriarchal (Fall/Redemption) Model

The Patriarchal Model (also referred to as the Fall/Redemption Model) has been the prevailing model in Western society for 1,700 years. For example, in business, leaders at the top tell the people down below what to do. The person or persons at the top carry all the power, and those below are considered to be servants. In this model, rewards go up the line. Those at the bottom are expected to work so that those at the top can prosper.

At the turn of the century, huge companies like Walmart generated billions of dollars in profit for those at the top. Walmart employees at the bottom, who were running the business, often had difficulty making ends meet on the salaries they received, while the executives at the top were making millions every year. Some of the goods sold by the company came from sweatshops in developing countries, where workers were treated like slaves.

The Patriarchal Model exists in almost every area of Western culture. In the medical field, drug companies generate enormous amounts of income, while people in need of their products must struggle to find money to purchase them. In education, costs are becoming prohibitive. In athletics, finance, communication, and even in religion, the people at the top make huge amounts of money while the people at the bottom barely have enough on which to live.

Whether you realize it or not, this Patriarchal Model is based on the way people relate to God! In 313 A.D., the Roman Emperor Constantine wanted to control more and more of the known world. He realized that he would be able to have much more power over the empire if everyone professed the same religion. For that reason, he decreed that Christianity would be the official religion of the Roman Empire (please note it was the person at the top telling the people down below what to do and how to believe).

At the same time, Constantine imposed the Patriarchal Roman Model on the Church. Before 313, the Christian Church commonly gathered in small communities. Generally, the faithful met in homes or other intimate spaces. After everyone arrived, the group would decide who was to lead the service. In this system, leadership of any religious service might change each time the community met, but the system clearly exhibited power from the bottom up, not from the top town. All members of these communities were considered equal, and authority was shared by everyone.

After Constantine imposed Roman patriarchal structures on the Church, power began to flow from the top down. Constantine began to have a say in the appointment of bishops and other Church leaders. In turn, Bishops began to appoint others into lower ecclesiastical positions. Even the liturgies for these appointments reflected the understanding that power was coming from God, down through the bishops, down through the priests, and eventually to the people.

St. Augustine, who lived at the end of the 300s, and who was heavily influenced by the structures created by Constantine, built his own spirituality on the model of the Romans. In his attempt to explain *his* spirituality, Augustine considered God to be up in the sky (above everyone). It was here, in the person of God, that he imagined all "good." In contrast, he saw human beings on earth (below God) as creatures in whom "evil" existed. In an effort to explain evil, he created the concept of "Original Sin." In *his* spirituality, all human beings are born with Original Sin and therefore are intrinsically evil. According to Augustine, therefore, the purpose of the Church was to help "fallen" human beings to find their way to God. Please note that Original Sin is a term created by St. Augustine to explain *his* spirituality. It is not an idea that Jesus knew.

Because Augustine was a very intelligent person as well as a powerful bishop in the Church, he became a great leader in his day and had a lasting influence on secular society, as well as on the Church, all the way into the 21st century.

If we were to diagram the spirituality of Augustine, in terms of his relationship to God, we could do it like this:

In this diagram, God is above and separated from human beings. Good is associated with God, and evil is associated with human beings. In this model, God is perceived as a law-giver who tells human beings what to do and a judge who rewards and punishes.

For 1,700 years in Western society, this model has been accepted in government (the "king" model); in education (teacher over student); in medicine (doctor in charge of the patient); in families (the father as "head" of the household); in business (the CEO giving direction to the entire company); in international relationships (one country seeking to dominate another); etc.

Attached to the Patriarchal Model are these characteristics:

1. Status quo refers to the striving to keep things as they are. For example, scientists, educators, and even some political leaders have been shouting that we have a crisis on our planet in terms of air pollution, water pollution, overpopulation, starving nations, etc. Yet government continues to leave things "as they are" and allows big business to continue polluting our air, our rivers, our streams, and our oceans (of course, for financial gain!). Little, if anything, is being done to stop the huge waste of food in some parts of the world while whole countries suffer starvation.

The same clinging to "status quo" exists in organized religion. In 1962 Pope John XXIII convened a Vatican Council. Theoretically, these Councils are the highest authority in the Church. This particular Council began a shift in spirituality, toward the Matriarchal Model. It stated repeatedly that the Church is the "People of God," not the hierarchy! It also called for "collegiality" in all levels of ecclesiastical government, recommended that members of religious orders get back to the ideals of their founders, that the Church get back to the ideals of Jesus, and that Catholics not only share their truth with other religious traditions, but also that they be open to the truth that is present in these other religious traditions. Unfortunately, leaders of the Church after the Council struggled to "keep things as they are" even when that choice was detrimental to the people and to our world. Renewal groups were requested by the Council, but these groups, still today, have challenges implementing change because of leaders who want to keep the "status quo."

The medical profession continues to use Newtonian physics instead of moving into the quantum model because the former is tied to the drug industry. Those in power fight to keep the "status quo," which generates huge income for the people at the top but is not always beneficial to the people at the bottom. (See Bruce Lipton's book *Biology of Belief.*)

2. Greed is another part of the Patriarchal Model. Business CEOs who are already very wealthy, wanting more and more, get involved in fraudulent activity that puts more money into their own pockets, of course at the expense of the poor who work for the company. Enron is a good example. Because the executives at the top were greedy for more money, they caused the company to collapse. As a result, employees at the bottom lost their jobs, and in many cases, their retirement, but the executives walked away with millions of dollars! Thank God, at this point, *some* of these offenders are being called to accountability.

The medical community, too, is getting more and more involved in economics, rather than in the healing process. I once heard a medical doctor talking to 20,000 educators at a national convention. He told us never to have an operation on the weight of only one doctor's diagnosis. He even went on to say that we should be especially careful when a doctor prescribes an expensive operation or procedure immediately before that doctor is going on vacation!

In organized religion also, there can be a preoccupation with money and the things that money can buy. A few years ago, I became aware of a church that cost $100 million. This project took so much money that 35 people in the office had to be "let go." The church became a monument to the person who built it at the cost of the staff who assisted the poor and the disadvantaged.

4. Dualism is also a part of the Patriarchal Model. Dualism refers to distinctions such as right and wrong, good and evil, us and them, male and female, body and soul, etc. Dualism is one way of looking at the world, but it is not a reality, it is a perception! When we make distinctions such as "us and them," we set up a system that says, "We are better, they are less!" This kind of thought process is at the base of all prejudice. In the United States, black people were brought from Africa as slaves and were considered property. This thought process affected every level of society, even church communities. It has taken more than 100 years to change this dualistic thought process and its negative effects.

The distinction made in the Patriarchal Model between male and female has created similar injustices. The Patriarchal Model is a male-dominated one. Males are considered higher on the hierarchical ladder, and for millennia, women have been forced to take, and remain in, subservient roles. Only in the very recent past has this dualism *begun* to change!

The dualistic model has also affected the way we look at ourselves. In the past we have made a distinction in human beings referred to as "body versus soul." Often in this dualism we were taught that the body is inferior (even evil) and that only the spirit is good. For this reason, individuals, even saints, punished their bodies to the point of physical harm. St. Francis, before he died, realized that he had done serious injustice to his body and begged his body for forgiveness! (See page 14, "Models for Relating," and compare other characteristics of the Patriarchal and Matriarchal Models.)

Before we move on, I want to mention that the Patriarchal Model is not always "bad." Sometimes, when used with love and compassion, it can be effective. For example, when children are growing up, parents can assume the authority of the Patriarchal Model because they realize that children are without experience and knowledge, and oftentimes must be protected and educated.

The Patriarchal Model will work when there is someone who wants to take the position of responsibility and power, and there are others who want to be "led." In marriage, for example, a kind and loving husband can be in charge of his wife (who is also kind and loving), but only a wife who is content to leave responsibility with her husband and who, at the same time, is willing to "serve" his every need. There are marriages like this that are happy and productive because the roles are clear, and the individuals involved are willing to "play" a particular role.

Mother Teresa is an example of a Patriarchal person. She had a clear mission and a specific lifestyle. Anyone wanting to join her community had to fit into the guidelines she created. I spoke to a young man who went to India to work with Mother Teresa. When he found that some of the people who were dying could be helped with simple medical assistance, he was told that the mission of the Sisters was to assist people who were dying, not to be involved in medical assistance.

The point I want to make is that one approach to spirituality is as good as the next, but as we will see later on, the movement in the 21st century is clearly in the direction of the Matriarchal Model.

The following are examples that I hope will help you understand more clearly how these models of spirituality appear in real-life situations.

John and Mary came from the same kind of background. In both of their families, the father was the head of the household and the wife subservient. When they married, each stepped into the roles they saw in their parents, and the marriage worked beautifully. Both came from the Patriarchal Model, chose to take their respective roles, and their relationship was successful. Their children also fit into the Patriarchal Model and grew up to be happy and stable individuals.

Gail and Peter came from different kinds of families. Peter's dad was the traditional patriarch and his mom the faithful servant, wife, and mother. Gail, however, came from a family where the roles were reversed. Gail's mother was the professional and the breadwinner. Her dad was a stay-at-home parent and raised the children. When Gail and Peter got married, they each went into the relationship thinking, "I will be the person in charge." Needless to say, after a short period of time, Gail and Peter were at odds with each other. Sometimes their differences of opinion resulted in heated arguments and hurt feelings. They never sought professional help and struggled in this relationship for over 30 years, until Gail died. Because the roles of the relationship were never clarified, the children were very confused. The oldest son did finally work himself into a stable marriage after several previous unsuccessful ones. The middle son got involved in drugs and never found a workable relationship. The third child became very successful in business but was never able to form a lasting relationship with any one person. In this family, both the husband and the wife were in the Patriarchal Model, but with each wanting to be in charge. Rarely does this kind of relationship work.

Alex and Pat both came from families where the mother and father had a relationship of equals. When they got married, they divided the responsibilities of the household (often exchanging those responsibilities to fit changing situations). If you were to ask either of them who was "in charge," they would ask, "Of what?" Both Alex and Pat consciously applied this approach of "equal" relationships by getting together every week and talking about what was working in the relationship and what was not working. They taught this approach to their children by having family meetings to make family decisions. The children grew up to be responsible and productive as well as unique and stable. They also proved to be good communicators. In this family, everyone functioned out of the Matriarchal Model to the benefit of all.

When one person comes from the Patriarchal Model and another person comes from the Matriarchal Model, there will be significant challenges in the relationship. George was a very capable, creative, and industrious person in business, where the Patriarchal Model was in place and in which George was very comfortable and successful as the boss. However, he was not able to build healthy relationships with his wife and children, who came out of the Creation Model. His wife, Rose, was a kind, loving, giving person who created wonderful loving relationships with everyone, including her children. In the early years of their marriage, Rose was the obedient wife, but as she began to get involved in programs for personal growth and development, she realized that she wanted to be a more independent person and get involved in areas of life that interested her. As soon as Rose began to create a new life for herself, George became angry (a controlling activity!). He wanted Rose to remain in the role of subservience to him. For many years, there was tension in the relationship until finally, George began to get involved in personal growth and development himself and moved into the

Matriarchal Model. The relationship today is wonderful because both are relating as equals in the Matriarchal Model.

3. Where Are You?

The above is all theory and may be interesting. However, for me, the important question is "What will I do with this theory? Does it have any practical use in real life?"

Personally, the distinctions created above have made a great difference in my life, or more correctly, have given me direction for my life. I very much want to be in the Matriarchal Model, but that is not an easy task. Like so many others, I have been brought up with strong Patriarchal training. That training cannot be removed from my personality as easily as taking off a coat! Change can take a good deal of time.

I am constantly looking for signs that will tell me whether I am using one model or the other. For example, anger is a sign, for me, of the Patriarchal Model. The other day, I picked up all the things that I wanted to take with me as I was preparing to run errands. With mail, a shoulder bag, an apple, a gym bag, and books in my arms, I tried to open the car door and, naturally, I dropped some of the items, which fell to the garage floor. I got angry and said things that I cannot print here. Of course, *I* was the problem, but I wanted to project the difficulty onto the things that I was carrying. I was angry because the things were not doing what I wanted them to do.

After that experience, I learned that I need to make two trips when I have too many items to carry to the car. That way I get the job done without having to get angry, and I can drive away from the house feeling calm and peaceful. I am getting better with experiences like these, but I still need to do some work to develop skills based on the Matriarchal Model!

In the same way, I am working on human relationships. When I find myself complaining about someone, criticizing, or even thinking about the shortcomings of another person, I stop and think, "Justin, you are unique, and others sometimes do not like the way you are, or the way you operate, so don't expect others to be the way you are!" I think of the times when I might have been like the person about whom I am talking, or thinking, and mentally say to myself, "I'm sorry, please forgive me." This kind of change in thought process helps me move further into the Matriarchal Model.

To be very honest, I must tell you that, at present, I have one foot in the Patriarchal Model and the other foot in the Matriarchal Model. I feel that I am doing a dance, moving from one model to the other, but I am getting better as time goes on. Slowly, slowly, I am moving into a space where I can feel I have "equal" relationships with myself, with others, with things, with life experience, and even with God. Developing the Matriarchal Model in my life is bringing more happiness and peace into my life. Try it! You'll like it

F. Application

1. "Should" is a word that we use to "push" others. Do you use it? How often?

2. "Don't you think that . . ." is another phrase that we use to let others know that we expect them to agree with what we are going to say. Do you use this phrase?
3. When you get angry, stop and ask yourself what, or who, are you trying to control.

4. When you function as a parent, teacher, pastor, policeman, etc., and it is appropriate for you to function from the Patriarchal Model, do you function in a kind and loving way?

5. As a student, child, spouse, employee, or friend, do you know how to say to someone in charge, "We need to talk?"

6. Pass on some good news about yourself, someone you dislike, someone with whom you are angry, someone to whom you have been unkind. Pay attention to how you feel afterward.

7. What is the most important thing that you have learned
    from this chapter?
    Share that information with another person. Talking
    about these ideas will anchor them in your subconscious
    and help you to learn them more quickly.

PRINCIPLE
1

There Is Beauty in Everyone and in Everything

Relationships exist in the world of Spirit. You cannot see or touch a relationship because it is something nonmaterial (or spiritual). Relationships, in fact, exist in the mind; they are creations of mind. (Remember, we are dealing with all relationships, those with self, as well as those with things, life experience, God, etc.)

Here are some illustrations. Mary Beth met Roger for the first time. She saw him as being physically attractive and engaged him in conversation. Roger asked Mary Beth about her work and seemed genuinely interested in listening to her. As they continue their conversation, Mary Beth realized that Roger is interested in many of the same things as she. His voice inflections, eye contact, body language, etc., led Mary Beth to believe that he is an honest person and someone she would like to know better. Because she was translating all of the communication from Roger in a positive way, she felt drawn to him, and from her point of view, the relationship is a positive one. Positive thoughts create positive relationships.

Jim is elderly but sees his cane as a sign of old age (which he despises!). He came out of a restaurant one morning with friends after an enjoyable breakfast. He made a negative comment about his "&$%# cane" and began a tirade on old age. His friend, Frank, in an effort to get Jim thinking in a more positive direction, described how an uncle used a cane as part of his wardrobe. The uncle had a brown cane for one set of clothing and a black one for other sets of clothing. Because he had a good relationship with his cane, this uncle always referred to his cane as a "walking stick" and saw it as something fashionable. Frank suggested that Jim view his situation in a more positive light, so that he could develop a better relationship with his cane and with his age.

Jim interpreted Frank's comment in a negative way and shouted in anger, "You have nerve making fun of an old man with a cane!" and went on to belittle this friend in front of the others who were there. Frank had no intention of making fun of Jim, but Jim's negative thoughts about his cane, about his friend's comments, and about his own age produced a negative experience that was uncomfortable and embarrassing for everyone present. Negative thoughts produce negative relationships.

In the following chapters, I want to share some principles which I believe affect all relationships. Of course, these are principles I have discovered for myself, and you may not agree with them, which is fine. I share them only because they help me create more positive relationships, and my hope is that they will help you develop more positive relationships too.

Looking at the universe from a scientific point of view, it is an amazing reality. Imagine, 13.7 billion years ago, a massive explosion called the Big Bang occurred. 10.5 billion years later our planet began to appear with its moon. Dinosaurs existed 250 million years ago, but humans arrived only 3 million years ago.

These timelines are mind-boggling and challenge our intelligence. Consider what we know of the universe: galaxies and stars, our planet and the atmosphere protecting it, the expanse of plant life and animal life, and the crown of earth life, you and me! Such magnificent beauty staggers human comprehension!

If you perceive the creation of the cosmos in this way, and pay attention to the details of daily life on our planet, you will see beauty everywhere! Every plant, every insect, every animal, every bird, every fish, yes, every human being is a magnificent creation manifesting the Infinite Beauty of the universe.

The mistake we humans make is to create a norm of our own, by which we judge something to be beautiful. This kind of thought process puts limits on beauty and consequently puts limits on our life experience.

For example, some people point to certain kinds of landscapes and call them beautiful and then point to other landscapes as ugly. Please note, this is the Patriarchal Model at work. The distinction between beautiful and ugly is arbitrary, created in someone's mind. However, the objective reality is that the universe (and everything in it) is beautiful. Yes, there is a great diversity covering the globe, but all of it is beautiful.

When I was teaching music at an all-boys' school, a wealthy person was giving away some items from his home. He gave a large painting to the school that eventually found its way to a wall in our music classroom. It was a painting of rough texture (actually sprinkled with sand), done in shades of gray, dark blue, and black. It depicted a group of young boys in the alleyway of a depressed part of the city. The boys were playing dice on the ground. It is a magnificent and powerful piece of art.

The average person looking down an alleyway in a depressed part of the city, seeing young boys on the ground playing craps, might reflect, "Isn't that awful? This is what makes our city ugly." *But* an artist can see the same scene from a completely different perspective and uses that image to create a piece of art. Positive thought creates a positive life experience. Beauty is in the eye of the beholder!

Often, I have been asked about what seems to be intrinsic evil, like war. Where is the beauty in something like that? Personally, I believe that war, in any form, is evil, but that is a moral judgment, not an aesthetic one. Yet, even in this kind of terrible experience, if you look deep enough, you will find beauty. Think of the American soldiers giving gum and candy to poor, deprived children, and you will see a scene of beauty. Or consider lifelong relationships that began in war camps between people on both sides of the fence, where prisoners befriended their guards. Or recall the photo and/or the sculpture of soldiers raising the American flag on Iwo Jima. Beauty is everywhere!

I was visiting with family in Las Vegas and, at a baptismal party, met a couple from Europe. Our discussion moved at one point to World War II. After discussing some of the negative aspects of the war, the wife turned the conversation in a completely different direction. "You know, Father," she said, "not everything about war is ugly." This statement was being made by a person who lived through the tragedy of war! With great interest, I asked, "What do you mean?" She went on to explain how during the war, life was very difficult. Food, shelter, and water were not always available, but inside the people who were living through this difficult life experience was a place of much love and compassion. Everyone was willing to help everyone else. Everyone was willing to share what little they had. Everyone became friends with everyone else. As love and compassion flowed between individuals of every age, religion, sex, culture, etc., there arose an atmosphere that was truly beautiful! At the end of her comments, she said, "I wish the society we live in today had that kind of love and compassion!"

In the Matriarchal Model, the belief is that all life experience is good, that God's plan is perfect, and that there are no mistakes. However, it is not always possible to see the whole picture immediately. Sometimes it may take years before all the pieces fall into place.

My dad was the last of 11 or 12 children. All of his brothers and sisters who married and who had children produced male offspring. When Daddy and Ma married, their first child was a girl! Imagine how important this child was to the entire extended family! At age 3, their little daughter, Mary Ann, was run over by a truck in front of our home and killed. Both of my parents went through a life experience that was, I suppose, as close as anyone could get to what some would call "hell." Ma told me that at one point, they had to tie her to a chair because she could not control herself in the grieving process.

After months of working their way through this difficult time, both Ma and Daddy wanted another child very much. That is when I came along! All the years I was growing up, Ma told her stories about Mary Ann to my brothers and me, showed us her pictures, and kept us in touch with the important memories that were treasured by her and many other members of the family.

When I was about 17, preparing to enter the seminary, I was downtown with Ma to get a plane ticket, and the conversation moved to our family history and to Mary Ann. In the middle of the conversation, Ma turned to me and said, "You know, Buddy, now that I look back, I think Mary Ann's death was the biggest blessing that God could have given to your dad and me." I was stunned by this comment and asked her to explain. She told me that when she and Daddy married, it was the year before the Great Depression. By the time their children were being born, she and Daddy put a lot of value in the house, the car, the money, and the good times. When Mary Ann died, however, all that changed. From that point on, the house, the car, the money, and the good times had little meaning. Their values completely changed, and what became most important was the family.

My folks dedicated their lives to putting love into our lives. Daddy began to read books on child psychology, and Ma radiated so much love that our house became a place of attraction for the entire extended family. Everyone enjoyed coming to our home, where we had music, singing, dancing, etc. At one such gathering, a young lady, who had come to the house for the first time, was watching my brothers and me saying good night to everyone. We boys had to go to each guest, give them a hug and a kiss, and say "Good night!" When I came to her, planting a kiss on her cheek and giving her a hug, she said to me, "You boys are so blessed to live in this house! I can feel the love reflecting off the walls!"

Years later, when I was studying spirituality, I was told to be in touch with my roots, especially the circumstances surrounding my birth. I decided to call Ma and get some details from her. On the phone, I asked her if she and Daddy were happy when they found out that she was pregnant with me. She said, "Buddy, you remember the story of Mary Ann. and how, after we got through the trauma of her death, your dad and I wanted another child?" I told her I remembered, and she said, "Well, once your dad and I got through the trauma of our loss, we wanted another child so badly." Then she added, "Buddy, you were loved before you were conceived!"

It is clear to me now why I have been preoccupied with the loving process all my life. I remember the excitement of being in church, at age 3, fascinated by the light filtering through the beautiful stained glass windows, the odor of candle wax and incense, the ornate altar with all the statues of saints and angels, and especially the feeling of love and peace that was always there among the people. At age 5, I knew my life's work would be as a Franciscan Friar because I saw how the Friars radiated love. Father Theobald Kalamaja, the pastor, was like a grandfather who not only talked about love but exuded love by his actions and his words. When he had to leave the parish to retire, a sadness fell over the entire congregation – something I remember to this day.

When I entered the Order, I found my spirituality fit, hand in glove, with the spirituality of St. Francis. My entire life has been driven to understand the loving process and to become a lover, the way Jesus, Francis, and my parents were. Now I travel the world teaching and spreading love the way I was taught by both my mom and my dad.

I would never be the person I am had it not been for Mary Ann's death and the change that event made in the lives of my parents and our family! This story took over 20 years to complete, and even though part of it seems tragic, as a whole it is beautiful, every part! Perhaps you will understand why I believe in this principle: *There is beauty in everything!* But the principle also says, *"There is beauty in everyone!"* Here is another family story to illustrate this part of the principle.

I think my mom was one of the most beautiful people in the world. Because love flowed from her so purely, everyone was attracted to her. After she died, I was sharing with my brother, Jack. He told me that Ma had a very poor self-image from the time she was a child. She told Jack that the happiest day of her life was her wedding day. She explained that she believed she was not attractive (speaking from a physical point of view) and that no one would ever ask her to marry. When I heard this from my brother, I understood why Ma never wanted to have her picture taken.

The most important part of this story comes from my dad. He told me that before he got married, he dated a lot of women. He was very handsome, worked for Western Electric, and did a lot of traveling. When he decided to marry, he returned to the old neighborhood to marry Ma, because, he said, "she was such a beautiful person!"

As time went on, Ma became involved in the family, the extended family, the neighborhood, and the church and began to feel much more secure about her person. When I was teaching Success: Full Living in the Omaha area, she always attended my classes, listening to me talk about how to build self-image and sometimes discussing that material with me. She began to shift her thought process and little by little gained more confidence and eventually became much more positive about herself. She even enjoyed having her picture taken!

Daddy and Ma on their Wedding Day

As an aside, I think that our society makes a great mistake in pointing to physical beauty as being the most important issue in relationships. What is even stranger is the foolish idea that beauty has to do with a slim body and particular facial features. Lasting beauty is within the person! All the years I was involved in helping young people prepare for marriage, I sought to help them see the *person* they were about to marry, not just a body! This distinction, I believe, is a major issue in determining whether a relationship will work or not. Parents, teachers, grandparents, pastors, counselors, etc., are in unique situations in which they can help young people to focus on this inner beauty, and not just on the outer reality.

Another consideration is helping young people to understand relationships. Years ago I attended a conference where a workshop was given by a nun and a priest. Both of them had years of experience working with teenagers. The workshop was created to help parents, teachers, clergy, and others working with teens to see life from the vantage point of 21st-century youth. In a role-playing sequence, the priest and the nun took the parts of teens. They were conversing with their parents: "Mom and Dad, we know about sex. Please tell us something about relationships." "Can you please tell us what it was like when you started dating?" "Tell us about your mistakes." "What was it like when you broke up with your first love?" "How did you know when you met the right person?"

If you train yourself to see beauty in every person you know, it will be a simple matter to teach others how to see this beauty. Especially parents, teachers, pastors, and those who work with children have a wonderful opportunity to teach this principle. If children make a habit of seeing beauty in others, think how easy it will be for them to do this as adults, and how enjoyable their lives will be (not to mention the difference it will make in our world)!

As a music teacher, I taught my students to look for beauty everywhere in their lives and in our world.

Every human being is a creative artist in one way or another because we all have the ability to see beauty in ourselves, in others, in the world around us, and in life experience. As artists, we can find beauty in places where most people cannot. Helping others see beauty is a great gift that we can give to our society, and it makes us valuable instruments for generating love and promoting peace.

I was teaching abroad, and into my class came an unusual couple. Jo, the wife, was a young nurse, and her husband, Jake, a paraplegic in a wheelchair. In the course of the weekend workshop, they told the story of how they met when Jake was in the hospital, how they fell in love, and how they found their way to a very successful marriage. Jo was the creative person who looked far beyond the limits of Jake's physical limitation and saw in him the exceptionally talented person he is. Jake, too, was able to develop a powerful and positive self-image and even today thinks creatively about their future and radiates a joy and peace everywhere he goes.

We are all creative artists in our own right, and when we tap into this unlimited reservoir of Mind, we can not only see beauty everywhere, we can also create it anywhere!

The goal of the Matriarchal Model of spirituality is to generate love and promote peace. This goal cannot be legislated from the top down; it is something that must come from the bottom up. Consider people like Gandhi, or Martin Luther King Jr., or Mother Teresa. They spoke very loudly by their example and were able to inspire thousands of others to follow their visions. You and I can be models too!

I believe the best place for everyone to start looking for beauty is within their own person. If you can see the beauty in you, it will be much easier to see beauty in others. For that reason, I offer the following exercise.

A. Personal Blessings

Your name: _____

List the blessings you have received during your lifetime (include personal items such as talents, accomplishments, personality traits, etc.):

1. _____

2. _____

3. _____

4. _____

You can make the list as long as you like. The idea is to focus on the assets in your person and in your life. I guarantee this exercise will help you create a better relationship with yourself.

In a workshop setting, students are able to pair off so that they can verbalize their lists to another person with explanation and details. The advantage of sharing with another person is that you can help yourself to be comfortable talking about the good things in your life, especially the good things in your person. Because it may not be possible for you to share immediately with another person as you read this book, I might suggest that you share these items with someone when you have the opportunity. Psychologically, it is healthy to see beauty both in your person and in your life, but doing this kind of reflection in conversation with others will anchor that reality in your subconscious. Developing a positive and loving relationship with yourself is not only valuable and important, it is essential for living a full life!

Once you can see beauty in yourself, it will be easier for you to see beauty in others. Unfortunately, the society in which we live generally comes out of a dualistic model. That means there is always an "us" and a "them." "We" are always "right," and "they" are always "wrong." We are taught to love those who love us and to hate those who make life difficult for us. It is this kind of spirituality that justifies enmity and war.

As a high school teacher I occasionally witnessed teen fights in the cafeteria. In one instance, John was returning to his seat after purchasing an ice cream cone. As he made his way through the tightly arranged tables and chairs, all crowded with students, he accidentally bumped into Pete, and the top scoop of his ice cream cone fell into the lap of Larry. Larry immediately sprang to his feet, shouting at the top of his voice, and began to physically attack John. Of course, John defended himself, and a fight ensued.

If you analyze the thought process, you will find it was something like this. As Larry reacts to the ice cream in his lap, he believes that John threw the ice cream with intent. John reacts, thinking that he is being unjustly attacked. The result is a fight. In this case, neither Larry nor John sees beauty in each other. Both see each other as enemies, and both justify the fight.

If we apply the Matriarchal Model to the situation, the thought process would be completely different. When the ice cream falls into Larry's lap and he jumps up brushing the ice cream off his trousers, he turns facing John, who, with his mouth opened, blurts out, "Excuse me! I'm sorry! It was an accident!" Larry sees the distress in John's eyes and says, "It's all right, as long as you share the rest of the ice cream with me!" Both boys begin to laugh, and others standing around hand Larry napkins to wipe off his trousers while others work to clean up the floor. Everyone walks away from the experience happy.

Please notice the thought process of the second example. Both John and Larry see and respect the beauty in each other. They make the best of an awkward and messy situation and create a positive result for everyone involved.

Thoughts are the controlling factor in every relationship. Positive, loving thoughts always bring positive, loving experience. This is especially true when two people go through a divorce. I know a wonderful lady, Peggy by name, who realized that she could no longer live with her husband. There were several children, and she knew divorce was going to be difficult for everyone. To help her husband through the difficult adjustment ahead, Peggy sat down with him often to talk about how the process could happen so as to make the adjustment as easy as possible for them, for the children, and for the families on both sides. She went so far as to postpone the divorce for a year so that her husband could better adjust. When the lawyer tried to get a disagreement going between Peggy and her husband, Peggy fired him and got another lawyer who was willing to work with her to keep all of the relationships intact, during and after the divorce. The process was long and challenging, but in the end, it worked out beautifully. Today the husband is remarried, and the entire family, including the husband's new wife, can be together for celebrations!

Dr. Elisabeth Kubler-Ross gave a presentation here in Indianapolis, which our center sponsored. Our staff was honored to have dinner with her at the Hermitage before she gave her presentation to the general public. During our conversation, she shared a beautiful story that also illustrates the Matriarchal Model in a real-life situation. After many years of marriage, her husband asked for a divorce. Dr. Kubler-Ross realized that the marriage had taken its course, and that she could not give her husband what he needed at that time in his life. With her blessing, he finalized the divorce and was remarried to a younger woman. When this new union generated a new addition to the family, Dr. Kubler-Ross was just as excited as the parents. She told us that somehow that baby was another grandchild, and she bonded with this child as she did with her own. She even offered to baby-sit when the parents wanted a night out. What wonderful example from all of these people, who continued to see beauty in every aspect of their lives, especially those that are difficult and challenging.

Dr. Kubler-Ross and Fr. Justin at the Hermitage

When individuals see beauty in everyone and in everything and seek to create and sustain love relationships; the result is always positive and rewarding.

My hope is that world leaders of government will come to understand this principle! The Matriarchal Model is reflected in the institution of the United Nations. Its purpose is to bring nations together, respecting their differences, looking for and celebrating the beauty in all their diversity. It is a wonderful beginning! Our challenge now is to educate world leaders into the Matriarchal Model of spirituality. When *leaders* can shift their thought process into an inclusive model, then the institution of the United Nations will be able to fulfill its mission. In this model, differences could be worked out around a table instead of on a battlefield! Peace is possible on our planet, but only when we begin to see beauty in every person, every nation, every religion, every culture, and in diversity itself!

If you want to begin the process of changing your thought process into the Creation Model, you might try the following exercise. Choose someone who is presently in your life, especially someone you dislike or someone you have allowed to offend or anger you. Begin looking for the good in that person and write down these items in the list below. Look for personality traits, talents, academic or business achievements, or the good things that you hear from others. You will find that as you create this list, your attitude will begin to change, and with a focus on the beauty in this person, you will find a love relationship beginning to grow. You may not believe this simple process can change your life, but I challenge you to try it!

B. Blessings of Another

Write the name of a person you dislike, someone you have allowed to anger or upset you, someone you see as being the cause of some personal pain, or someone with whom you would like to improve your relationship. This could also be a government official, a church leader, a boss, a teacher, etc.

Name: _____

Every day, list the good things you have discovered about this person: personality traits, talents, financial or business accomplishments, or good things that you have heard from others.

1. _____

2. _____

3. _____

4. _____

5. _____

6. _____

You can make the list as long as you like. The idea is to focus on the person's personal assets. I guarantee this exercise will help you create a better relationship with this person and bring more peace and love into your life.

I, personally, used this exercise on the person of Saddam Hussein. I had created a very negative attitude toward this man because of all the "bad news" I heard from the media. I started to look for the good and discovered things that helped me see a person other than the dictator-assassin.

I had the opportunity to live in the Middle East and became friends with a good many Arabs. I don't understand some of their values and customs, but I do know that women in some of these communities are considered to be unimportant, even to the point of disposable. I say this because I worked with some loving, dedicated Polish nuns on the Mount of Olives in Jerusalem. They staffed an orphanage for female babies who, in some cases, were literally thrown away because they were female.

Then, I discovered that Saddam Hussein adopted a daughter. In my estimation, that was an heroic thing to do, if you put it within the context of the Arab culture. I saw an interview with Saddam's wife, who spoke of his love for this child and how tender he could be with her and with others in the family. She said that she could not understand how people could dislike her husband because he was such a loving person.

I began to realize that there was a positive side of Saddam's person, and this perception helped me to create a more balanced image of him and helped me to rid myself of judgment and anger. As I put this information together with the terrible childhood of this man, I could understand him a bit more and began, in my meditations, to send him love and healing. At that point, my life became more calm and peaceful!

C. Application

1. Accept All Persons (Including Yourself) and All Life Situations as Beautiful, Exactly as They Are

It is easy to apply this directive when people and life are giving you pleasant experiences. In the Gospels Jesus said: "If you love only those who love you, what reward will you have? Do not even the tax collectors do the same thing?"

The challenge comes when you have to deal with people who are difficult or with life situations that are painful. In my first book, *Success: Full Living,* I shared my belief that all life experience is good – all of it! The observation that I made there was that some life experience is pleasant – and some of it is not so pleasant – but all of it is good. Our society, however, makes us believe that pleasant experiences are good and unpleasant experiences are bad. In my estimation, this statement is false. My experience tells me that although pleasant experiences are good, unpleasant experiences of life are the most valuable. It is the unpleasant, challenging, and sometimes even painful experiences that give us the greatest opportunities for personal growth and development.

A tiny child can accept all the ease, all the joy, all the comfort, all the happiness of life. You don't have to be mature for that! But to accept difficulties, to work with them, and to overcome them are the very means by which we grow and mature, become better human beings, and acquire more insight into the meaning of life.

I was living with a Friar who had a very negative outlook on life. He was constantly complaining about other Friars in the community, moaning about the workload he had, and giving the impression that he was more burdened with responsibility than anyone in the world. It was as if he had a sign on his forehead that said, "Poor me. Pay attention to all the pain and suffering in my life!" It was not pleasant being with this Friar!

I decided that I needed to apply the above principle if I wanted to create a more positive experience for myself. I began to make a conscious effort to share all the "good news" I could with him. I congratulated him on any success that he had in his work. I supported him in the challenges he had dealing with illness in his immediate family. I helped him to see the blessings all of us were experiencing in community. I even made a point of going to some of the other Friars to share the good things I discovered about him. This project motivated me because I knew it was helping me become a better person. I noticed that my efforts helped *me* feel better about the Friar with whom I was working and even saw some positive change in him. At one point, one of the Friars told me, "Justin, when you are around, he seems to be a different person! He even smiles!"

If you are interested in creating a more positive life experience for yourself, looking for beauty in your own life can help a great deal. I am adding here another exercise that I hope will help you find beauty in any life experience.

2. Insight into Life Experience

a. Describe an event from your life when you were very happy.

_____

_____

_____

_____

_____

How did this event *help* your personal growth and development? How did this event *limit* your personal growth and development?

_____

_____

_____

_____

_____

b. Describe an event from your life when you were very unhappy, sad, or depressed.

_____

_____

_____

_____

_____

How did this event <u>help</u> your personal growth and development? How did this event *limit* your personal growth and development?

_____

_____

_____

_____

_____

3. Share Only the Good That You See in Others

At the time of this writing, I am in the midst of one of the most contested presidential elections in the history of the United States. I am very aware of how I feel when I turn on the TV and listen to "bad news" about both candidates. When I am in conversation with friends and family, I feel as though I am being pushed in one direction by those who are Democrats and in another direction by those who are Republican. What I find interesting is that most often I am being told why I must *not* vote for a particular candidate. I get long lists of "bad things" that will happen if I vote in that direction. In some cases, the list is so long that I begin to feel fear! But I must admit that I get the same treatment from people on the other side of the fence. All of this negativity could cause me to feel depressed, if I allowed myself to believe what I am being told.

What I do in my own thought process is to look toward the future and ask myself, "Which candidate do I believe has what is needed to move our country and the world into a better place?" I am then forced to look at the positive qualities of the candidates, and that makes me feel much better.

Voting in our Order is such a different experience! When we have to consider candidates for the office of Minister Provincial, the highest office in our Province, we use a completely different approach. Those who feel called to this kind of responsibility are asked to speak to the entire Province when we are gathered for a Provincial Convocation. Each candidate is asked to speak to his qualifications and to his vision for the Province and the Order. There is no place in our structure for "attacking" another candidate! The process is entirely positive, but at the same time thought-provoking, and allows for discussion and discernment among all the Friars in the Province. We put our attention on the talents of the candidates and look for the one who would best bring our Province and our Order into a better place. Elections in our Order are, for me, uplifting and positive experiences.

If you are serious about making your life more satisfying, try one of the following exercises for a day and then pay attention to how you feel:

a. Share Some Good News about Yourself or about What Is Going on in Your Life

You don't have to be conspicuous or move into the mode of bragging. For example, yesterday I got a phone call from one of my students who really appreciates what I have taught and what I believe in. She is helping others to know about my presence and about the work of the Hermitage. It makes me feel good to know that something that I have said or taught has made a difference in someone's life! This may seem like something small to you, but after sharing good news with anyone, we both leave the conversation feeling better. Sometimes my sharing sparks the memory in the other person to share something positive from his or her life! That's when the positive energy really begins to flow!

At our weekly Energy Circles at the Hermitage, one of the most important things we do is share our "success stories". This exercise helps to move the energy of the group in a positive direction, but it also helps us to recall and share the good things that make our lives full. My hope is that weekly sharing like this will help the participants develop the habit of thinking about and sharing the good news of our lives and our world. The more blessings we share each day, the more blessings there are!

b. Share Some Good News about Someone You Dislike

St. Therese, the Little Flower, was really good at this practice! She was in a convent working with another Sister whom she disliked very much. She made a point of sharing only the good things she knew about this particular Sister. She was so effective with this exercise that the Sister she was talking about approached her one day and asked, "Sister, why is it that you have such love and affection for me?"

In our society, this positive approach is not modeled very often. In fact, if you look at humor in our society, you will find that much of it is negative "put downs." Youngsters who are being exposed to this kind of approach become skilled with "put down" language early on. Grade school children can be brutal with this kind of language directed at fellow students. What is so tragic, in my estimation, is that these children and young adults do not realize that this kind of behavior lessens their own value as human beings and pushes them into a lifestyle that can become very limited, unhappy, and unhealthy.

One of my students at the high school level was an outstanding person. He was kind, gracious, respectful, and responsible, but with only average academic ability. Because he was a gentleman, supportive of fellow students, always willing to help others, and sensitive to their needs, he was elected president of his class for both his junior and senior years. When he graduated, the school administration named him "Mr. Bruin," the highest award a student could achieve! He went on to become successful in college and in life. What a wonderful example of someone who knew how to see the good in others and reflect it back to them!

Parents, teachers, pastors, or anyone working with youngsters can be powerful examples for children and young adults by simply modeling these ideals. At one point in my teaching career, I was in class and, as an aside, complimented one of my students on his vocal ability. Years, later, I was doing a class in New York City, had completely forgotten about this particular student, and received a phone call from him. He invited me to have dinner with him, and we set a time to meet at a particular restaurant. While I sat at a reserved table, waiting for him, music began to play and he appeared in costume to sing the famous aria *Vesti la giubba* from Leoncavallo's *Pagliacci.* I was completely overcome listening to this young student, singing with such professionalism and emotion. During our dinner, he told me that when I made that comment in class, so many years earlier, he decided then and there to get serious about his singing. I had lost track of him, but he never forgot me and what I said to him that day in class. Passing on awareness of the good you see in others not only affects the other person but also becomes rewarding for you!

c. Share Some Good News about Someone with Whom You Are Angry

I received a phone call from Mark, a friend I had known for half of my life. Without my being able to say anything in my defense, he accused me of what he obviously considered to be something very serious, but something about which I knew nothing. He didn't allow me to say anything, and when he finished speaking, he hung up. I was stunned and, after much thought, decided to write a letter to say that I did not deliberately do anything to offend him and asked for forgiveness if I did. I continued to keep in touch with Mark, sent birthday cards, Christmas gifts, etc., but I never got a reply. This was one of the most wonderful persons I have ever met. He is a giving, talented person whom I admire and respect and whose ability with people is something I will envy for the rest of my life. I just could not understand the seeming contradiction

Among some of the most moving things I know about Mark took place many years ago. He had spent a good deal of his life working to support his mother and brother. Most everything he earned as a teenager, he gave to the family for food, shelter, entertainment, etc. He did, however, put money aside for himself and purchased the home in which the family lived. His job eventually took him to another city, so he allowed his brother and mother to live in the house with the understanding that they would make the mortgage payments in lieu of rent. He came back to visit on a regular basis, but preferred living in the city where he worked, and where he was able to build a very comfortable existence for himself. Mark joined a religious community, made many friends, and used his skills to help others however he could.

When his mother was getting up in years, she wrote to him, telling of problems that they were having with the roof of the home. It was going to cost a great deal to replace the entire roof, but the mother suggested that the house be put in her name because, as a senior-owner, she could get government aid to replace the roof. She then told Mark that after the roof had been repaired she could put his name back on the deed. The son was hesitant, and the mother countered by saying, "You can't trust your own mother?" So Mark signed the house over to his mother.

The Christmas after the roof was completed, Mark returned home and asked his mother to sign the house back over to him. She refused, saying that it was the only security she had. Mark simply said: "Mother, I forgive you!"

Even when his mother died and Mark found out that the house was willed to both him and his brother, Mark still did not carry anger or resentment toward his mother.

When I think of the love that Mark had for his family, I can forget about the fact that I was unjustly accused, and am able to give Mark the kind of forgiveness he gave his mother. Positive thoughts produce a positive life experience!

d. Share Some Good News about Someone to Whom You Have Been Unkind

Many years ago, I did something very stupid that offended a good friend of mine. I tried to explain that it was a mistake, that I was sorry, and that human weakness was involved. However, he would not forgive me, and, of course, I felt very badly about the entire affair. I lost a friend because of this incident, but ever since then, I remember and talk about only the good experiences I've had with him and his family. I did all I could, admitting my mistake, offering my apologies, and asking for forgiveness. I accept the consequences of my actions and carry no grudge.

At one point, I was writing letters to people I had offended and once again approached this friend, but I never got a reply. I have since let go of the entire situation, and whenever I think of him I send my love and healing via meditation. By being positive, I feel I am "off the hook" as long as the door of my love is open! I refuse to say anything negative about him or the situation and I am at peace. I learned a long time ago that love is our destiny, and everything else is of little consequence. *Principle 1, There is beauty in everyone and in everything,* can help you understand this important truth!

.

PRINCIPLE
2

You Can Change Yourself – You Cannot Change Others

In my first book, *Success: Full Living*, I explained a system that I call the "Life Mechanism." This concept shows how choice of goals and attitudes creates a person's life experience. If you choose to have a positive attitude and/or if you choose goals that are appropriate for you, you will create a satisfying life. However, if you choose to have a negative attitude and/or choose a goal that is not appropriate for you, you will create a dissatisfying life, *but the choice is always yours!*

The Life Mechanism that is present in your person is the same mechanism that is present in every other human being. That means we all make our own choices in life, and we cannot blame our choices on anyone else! Statements like "It's her fault" or "The devil made me do it" are always false.

A. Relating to Life Experience

When it came time for me to go to high school, I wanted to go to the seminary because I knew that my destiny was to be a Franciscan priest. However, both of my parents thought otherwise. My dad, I think, believed that if I went to high school at Creighton Prep in Omaha, Nebraska, I would forget about becoming a Franciscan priest. My mom still carried the loss of my sister and told me sincerely, "Buddy, if you really have a vocation, four years won't made a difference to *you*, but having the family together for those few years will make a great difference to *me*."

I made the choice of taking the entrance exams at Prep and failed. My dad was sure that I had flunked purposefully so that I could go to the seminary. Because my older brother, Jack, had already successfully completed his first year at Prep, my dad approached the principal and requested that I have the opportunity to take the exam again. Even though I passed the exam, my preference was not Creighton Prep, but because of my folks, I chose to go – it was my choice, although a difficult one.

I must admit, however, that deep down inside, I knew everything would work out. Even though I did not feel I "fit in" at the school, I believed this was the route God wanted me to take.

When I finally did arrive at the seminary for two years of junior college, I saw the seminary high school situation firsthand. Looking back from that vantage point, I don't know if I would have been able to survive the high school seminary situation! In any case, I knew it had been more appropriate for me to go to high-school in Omaha and not at the seminary. In this situation, I was able to apply *Principle 1, There is beauty in everyone and in everything.* At the same time, I could understand *Principle 2, You can change yourself – you cannot change others.* I made the choice to follow the desires of my folks. They did not force me to make the choice, I made it freely. The result was a satisfying life experience.

B. Relating to Things

Principle 2 also applies to relationships with things. For me, this statement is obvious when I am working with my computer. I can choose to think of my computer as a "friend" that helps me to be efficient in my work, creates organization in my life, and allows me to communicate easily and quickly with people all over the world. When I make this kind of choice, my relationship with my computer feels good, and I enjoy sitting down to work with it. However, I must admit, sometimes I have made other choices when relating to my computer.

When I first began using a computer, I was working on a book and had completed a chapter. I really felt happy and satisfied with the results. When I went to save it, I chose the wrong command and deleted the entire chapter. I was furious, saying unprintable things about the computer. Now that I look back, I realize that I made a choice that was not appropriate for the result I wanted. There was nothing wrong with the computer; it did exactly what I told it to do. The error was mine, not the computer's.

Since then I have learned to more consistently use *Principle 2, You can change yourself – you cannot change others.* Just yesterday, I wanted to save a story that was e-mailed to me, but I didn't want to save all of the addresses that were attached to it, so I tried to delete them. The computer would not allow me to do that, so I thought I would copy the story into a Word document and then save it. When I tried to do that, the computer would not take the entire article; it took only one page at a time. I could have gotten angry, as I did in the past, but I know now that the computer is programmed to work in a particular way, and if I don't know how to give it commands that it understands, it will not function the way I want it to function. Anger will do nothing to change the computer; it will only create an unpleasant life experience for me.

I have come to understand that when I don't know enough to give the appropriate commands to the computer, I consult with Brian, our computer person, and he helps me understand how the computer works, so that I can use it appropriately. Using Principle 2 has brought a lot of peace into the relationship I have with my computer!

C. Relating to Others

Of course you can apply Principle 2 in relationships with people. Years ago, when I was still immature, I thought of myself as being the norm, and believed that my viewpoint was the correct one for everybody (the Patriarchal Model was alive and well in my life at that time!). As a young high school teacher in the music department, I knew that music was important in the lives of my students, in much the same way that music is important in my life. I believed that I could force my students to learn and to appreciate music as I did. With that attitude, I went into the classroom taking the role of a dictator. Needless to say, I created reactions that were less than favorable!

At that time, I had a wonderful young assistant by the name of Carole. She was talented, creative, and someone with whom I could talk easily. I told her that I wanted the students to get the exciting experiences from music that I had gotten all of my life, but "pushing" was not effective. We discussed the situation and began to look at the classroom from the viewpoint of the students. Our question was this: How can we capture the attention of the students from the very beginning? What kind of experiences would they enjoy, and, at the same time, motivate them to want to return to the music classroom?

After a good deal of discussion and creative thinking, we came up with the idea of creating a "happening." We would use only the accepted classical compositions that would be studied in the course, but we were going to put a creative twist to the experience. We recorded bits and pieces of classical works and created a 40-minute musical background. We decided to use the small auditorium, on the ground level of the school, because of the added space that was available there. We began with a march by John Philip Sousa and got the students marching around the room. In the meantime, I went to the projection room, removed my religious habit, and joined the group in secular clothes. We then used a bit of jazz, and Carole appeared on the stage as a "flapper" from the 1920s, swinging her beaded bag and moving creatively to the music. We added a Strauss waltz to which Carole and I danced on the stage; we used the *1812 Overture* while students, who had balloons, popped them in time with the cannons at the end of the composition.

On and on it went for 40 minutes. – I must say the students were totally captivated and left the room with great excitement about this compulsory general music class!

This project was so successful that I shared it at a Music Educators Association meeting. Other teachers became interested and enthusiastic, thinking how they could use some of these ideas in their own classrooms. The president of the association approached Carole and me, asking if we could do some kind of follow-up to the program, perhaps a research paper. When the paper was completed, it was published in the National Catholic Music Educators Association's *Research Bulletin.* In the weeks that followed, Carole and I got letters from people all over the world asking about the project and its success.

When Carole and I realized that we could not change the way our students thought, *but* that we could change the way *we* thought, we were able to communicate much more effectively with the students. Making that shift in our thought process made it possible for us to create not only something valuable for ourselves and our students, but also something that would be helpful for teachers around the globe.

Principle 2, You can change yourself, you cannot change others worked beautifully for us!

D. Relating to the Cosmos

One of the massive changes taking place in our lives in the 21st century is the way we look at the cosmos. For thousands of years, we spoke about the universe as it is described in the Book of Genesis. This viewpoint is primitive, because it was created by a primitive people. In this model, the Earth is perceived as being flat and supported by pillars. The pillars are set in water below the underworld. Pillars support the heavens and the firmament (a dome) keeps the water above the earth from falling down and destroying the earth. God lives above the firmament (in heaven), and it is this God who allows rain and snow to fall through the holes in the firmament to water the earth. Sun and moon were thought to travel across the firmament to create day and night.

It is this perception of the cosmos that is responsible for the prayers we still use in our liturgies today: "God in Heaven....."; "Heavenly Father, look down on your children. . . "; etc. It is this perception of cosmic reality that created the image of Jesus coming down from heaven and ascending into heaven to be reunited to the Father.

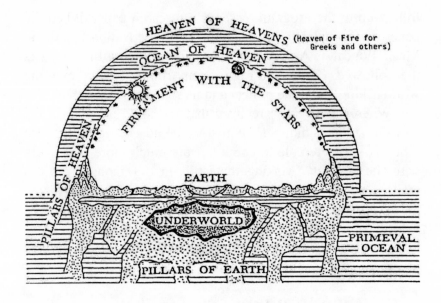

A Common Cosmology of the Ancient World

In the 20th century, our image of the cosmos changed dramatically. Now, in the 21st century, scientists not only describe the beginning of the universe using the image of the Big Bang, they also date that event at approximately 13.7 billion years ago. From this major cosmic event, everyone and everything has emerged. Even more astounding is our awareness that the universe continues to expand and develop.

As dramatic as these changes may seem, they still allow for a Universal Intelligence (or a God Presence) that powers the continuous creation of new stars and galaxies, as well as all life forms, including our own. However, this shift in our perception will demand a change in the way we think about ourselves and our relationship with God. We can no longer perceive God as assembling the earth and then putting humanity into it. New scientific information suggests the image of God creating the Big Bang, and from that event come the universe and all living creatures in it. With this shift of perception, Creative Intelligence operated in every atom and electron, in dark matter and in black holes, in every living cell and the creatures formed by those cells.

Our Milky Way Galaxy
(Its diameter is 100,000 light years across!)

Let me remind you that spiritual realities do not change because we have new information about the material world. What changes is the way we talk about spiritual reality. As you already know, we cannot adequately express anything in the spirit world because language is finite and the spirit world is infinite. Past expressions of Spirit have been inadequate, as are the expressions of the present. However, every generation brings with it deeper insight into spiritual reality. That process continues as we move into the future. (See *The Awakening Universe* by Neal Rogin.)

For decades, theologians have been working to find appropriate language to integrate the new cosmology with theological truth. As you might imagine, those who are not educated in the new cosmology, whether they be in leadership positions or not, always feel threatened by new language and changing liturgical expressions. Their discomfort, however, will not stop the development of scientific studies and the consequent emergence of new theological insight.

In the 1600s we had this kind of major change in cosmology when Copernicus and Galileo taught that the sun was the center of our system. Church leaders believed that the earth was the center of the universe and refused to change their minds, even though Galileo presented mathematical and scientific proof. Galileo was found suspect of heresy, placed under house arrest, and his movements restricted by the Pope.

Today we have a similar challenge. Leadership in every field - government, medicine, organized religion, education, etc., are being challenged with massive changes in our perception of the world.

When government leaders come to the awareness that all human beings come from one source, they will be forced to create systems of equality. The fact is we are one family. We are a global village where justice and freedom are due every man, woman, and child, every plant and animal, as well as every resource needed to sustain life on this planet. Political leaders are being forced to seek solutions by using dialogue instead of war, by building working relationships with all nations, and by creating systems that work in every corner of the globe.

Medicine, today, is becoming more grounded in quantum physics and the holographic model of the universe (instead of biology and chemistry). That means healing methodologies are built on energy instead of drugs. Medical professionals are creating new, more effective, and less invasive healing strategies and procedures. Eastern systems like acupuncture and acupressure, as well as homeopathy, are commonly used all over the planet. Electronic devices like Wellness Pro are rebuilding damaged body tissue and organs, as well as opening doors for cancer and AIDS cures. Meditation is clearly moving into the medical picture, as well as support systems like 12-step programs.

In organized religion, Scripture scholars are being challenged to clarify the difference between fact and myth. Traditionalists who continue to think in terms of the old cosmology, find themselves at odds with those who accept the new cosmology. Prayer in the new cosmology changes to forms like this one, by a well-known Catholic priest:

A Psalm of Cosmic Communion
by Fr. Ed Hayes

May I join you, cosmic congregation of galaxies,
as you dance with delight before our God.
You spin and leap with brilliant bursts of light,
 never tiring of your sacred circle-play.

May I join you, star-children of countless constellations,
in the worship of our common Creator
in your rotating rituals of nuclear energy
as you sing cosmic chants of divine fire.

May I join you, I who find my times of devotion
so often flat and fireless,
bound by routine and uninspired,
stagnant due to their lack of zeal.

May I join you, so that my prayers
may also spin with sparkling splendor,
spawning long tails of luminous devotion
to carry my praise and adoration
straight to the heart of my Beloved God.

In the Catholic Church, we have always believed that faith builds on nature. That means we have to use valid scientific information about nature and build our faith on that knowledge. We cannot ignore what science has to say about the material world, in the same way that the scientific community cannot ignore what the theological community has to say about the spiritual world.

Personally, I am fascinated by the new cosmology. It creates for me a vision of Divine Power that is beyond anything that I could have imagined previously. With these new images I have an awareness of God's greatness which is mind-boggling, an awareness that puts me into a mental state of tremendous awe!

With this new insight, I know that all living things are related, that there is only one Source of life, and that the teaching of Jesus about universal love is valid. Were I to refuse the understanding that comes from scientists at this point in time, this deeper spiritual awareness would not be a part of my living experience.

Now more than ever, with change happening so quickly in our world, I feel it is essential that I open my mind to new thought and expanding realities, to see humanity as the crown of God's creation, to know that I am the Universe Knowing Itself, and to assume the responsibility of protecting and nurturing all of nature and the universe. What a fantastic opportunity we have in this day and age to experience reality in a way few human beings in the past have been able to experience it.

I believe that, for the first time in human history, we, the rank and file, are able to "see" reality the way Jesus did, the way the Buddha did, the way Krishna did, the way the prophets did! With this cosmic awareness, it becomes much easier to understand why we are challenged to love one another because when we love others, we are enhancing our own lives. When we work with the "green movement," we are protecting the environment that is necessary to sustain our lives on this earth. When we work with others in the direction of world peace, we are generating the God Presence in our world, and in our lives. I believe that when human beings know the universe in this unitive way, then will we have reached our destiny.

The challenge for all of us is to take responsibility for changing *ourselves.* Each of us has a responsibility to pay attention to Mother Nature, to the Inner Reality of personal, spiritual experience, and to live what we believe – always within the context of love.

All of the above is another application of *Principle 2, You can change yourself – you cannot change others.*

E. Relating to Others of Different Beliefs

I was giving a lecture to a large number of people about meditation, as described in my book *Success: Full Thinking.* In the middle of the lecture, a young man stood up waving a book in his hand titled *The Beautiful Side of Evil.* Speaking not only to me, but to the entire audience, he shouted that meditation was dangerous because it opened people's minds to demons, that I was leading unsuspecting audiences into devil worship, etc. I explained to the young man that I was familiar with the book, but that I could not address it in my lecture, because the audience was there to hear what I had to say about meditation and the class that I was preparing to present. I told him that I would be happy to discuss the book with him in private, after the lecture, but he was insistent that I do it as part of the lecture. The audience became annoyed and asked him either to sit down and be quiet or to leave.

After the lecture, I made an appointment to see this young man the following day, and when he arrived at the office, he was carrying a stack of books. He introduced himself as John, and I began our conversation by asking about his background. He had been raised Catholic, but he was now in a fundamentalist church, where he learned about the dangers of meditation. I asked if he believed what I was teaching was dangerous, and without hesitation, he answered, "Yes!" I then explained that I could accept his belief, and that if I were he, I would not get involved in the program; but I also explained that I believed I was offering to my audience the very tools that would help them communicate better with God. I knew our beliefs were different, that I could accept where he was, and asked him to accept where I was.

John knew, at that point, that any logic or argumentation was futile. He simply had a different belief than I did, and the only thing we could do was to accept each other where we were and go on with our lives. Applying *Principle 1, There is beauty in everyone and in everything,* I could understand where John was on his journey. (I was in the same mindset when I was younger!) At the same time, I knew that John would not be able to understand where I was, at least not at this point in his life journey. Our challenge was to apply *Principle 2, You can change yourself, you cannot change others,* accept each other where we were, generate a love relationship, and live together in peace.

The following incident in my life is another example that helped me better understand Principle 2. I moved from high school education into a retreat center where the Friars welcomed me with open arms. They supported the programs I created and immediately helped me build a teaching ministry. Everything was going beautifully until there was a change of staff. Two of the Friars moved to continue their ministries elsewhere, and I was asked by the Provincial Office to take over the leadership of the center. Soon after, several other Friars joined our staff, one who was of a rather fundamentalist mindset and who did not appreciate my approach to Franciscan spirituality – nor did he agree with the meditation techniques that I was teaching.

Without my knowledge, several of these Friars complained to our Provincial Leadership, and without any consultation with me, the Provincial sent a letter from headquarters telling me to take my programs elsewhere. In all my years in the Order, I never knew a Friar to be sent *away* from a friary; we are always transferred *to* a new assignment.

I was devastated by this letter! The programs that I was offering at the center for five years were responsible for most of the income that supported the center, and without any consultation with me, the Provincial Leadership simply said, "Leave!"

One of the secretaries volunteered to join me in this move. A Methodist minister who had been in my classes, and who was interested in retreat work, also volunteered to assist in creating a center elsewhere.

I was allowed to take the income from the class I was teaching at the time I received the letter, but I was not allowed to take anything else. The night I left the friary was one of the most painful experiences of my life!

On the other hand, my students were most supportive! One, a Jewish gentleman, without my knowing anything about it, had started a fund, several years earlier, to support my work. When he learned of my situation, he presented me with a check for $5,000. Other students, from all over the country, sent financial gifts, and in a short while we set up an office, created a dedicated staff, and were off and running with what is now the Franciscan Hermitage.

During all this time, I was meditating daily to keep anger and resentment out of my mind and out of my life. I thought to myself, "Justin, you teach love and compassion. You have to become proficient at it now!" So, every day, three times a day in meditation, I sent love and healing to everyone who was responsible for the changes that made the Hermitage a reality.

Somehow in the quiet of my meditations, I knew that everything was in Divine Order, and within a short time, I was thrilled to know that, with the help of others, we had created an inter-faith center that would give us all the freedom that we needed to continue our work, both here and abroad. In fact, all of the staff members were able to feel grateful for everyone and everything that helped us to create the Hermitage.

We came to realize that we could not change the thought process of those whom we had left behind, but we could shift our own thoughts, visualize our productive and influential future, and move on with joy and excitement.

We came to understand Principle 1 a little better: *There is beauty in everyone and everything.* But we also were able to apply *Principle 2, You can change yourself– you cannot change others.*

Ironically, when the Hermitage was only about six months old, the Provincial from our Province came for his annual visitation. When he saw the daily prayer schedule we kept, the regularity of our monthly days of recollection, and the time we put aside for annual retreat, he asked me to share our ideals and prayer schedule at a regional meeting of the Friars. His comment was, "This is the kind of prayer schedule I would like to see in all of our friaries."

Ever since that time, the leadership of the Sacred Heart Province has offered the Hermitage constant moral and prayerful support. We are respected for our programs, our dedication, our creativity, and for what we are doing to promote inter-faith projects of many kinds - projects that are helping to generate world peace.

F. Relating to Sexuality and Gender Issues

A very important area of change in our world is the way we perceive sexuality and sexual diversity. In the past, we were told that there is only one category and that is heterosexuality. Any other lifestyle is a deviation and morally wrong. This teaching was clear and simple.

Today, however, in the 21ˢᵗ century, the scientific community is making it clear that sexuality, sexual categories, and gender are very diverse. I attended a workshop given by a priest and a nun who were professionals in this field. They explained the scientific studies that plotted all of humanity on a continuum with homosexuality at one end and heterosexuality at the other end. These studies show that, at one end of the continuum, 10 percent of the population are entirely homosexual. At the other end, 10 percent of the population are entirely heterosexual. In the center, 10 percent of the population are bisexual. What is more interesting is that the rest of the human population is equally scattered along this continuum, some having a major in one direction and a minor in the other direction while others, on the other side of the continuum have a major in the opposite direction and a minor in the other direction.

Perhaps this diagram will help to illustrate this continuum:

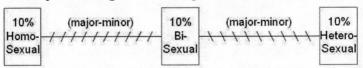

But this outline is not complete. Separate from these groups is another category of persons who are asexual. These are persons who have no sexual attraction to either male or female persons. The studies show that the asexual category represents 15 percent of the total population, 14 percent of whom are women.

Still, this is not the complete picture either, because now we have the categories of transsexual and intersexual persons (who carry physical organs of both male and female), as well as transvestites. The following diagram shows sexual orientation and gender to be much more complex that we have ever imagined.

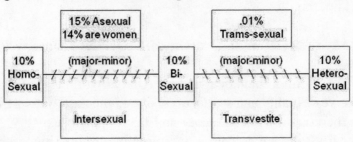

Thank God, at this point in time, we are beginning to recognize the wonderful diversity that God has created! Knowing that this diversity is natural and an important part of the creative hand of God, we may soon be able to accept all human beings as they are, and not try to force them into human-made categories, as we have in the past.

Some years ago, I was attending a conference on sexuality, and the attendees got involved in a very spirited discussion about all of the above. Toward the end of the evening, the moderator noticed an elderly American Indian woman, who happened to be seated next to me. He asked this wonderful lady to share what approach was taken in her tribe. She stood up and said, "I don't understand why you create categories and then force people into them. In our tribe, if someone is born and does not fit the categories we have, we create a new category. At present, we have 16 categories."

If the reader is interested in getting further information about this important topic, I highly recommend a DVD that was published by the National Geographic Society titled: *Sex, Lies, and Gender* as well as publications by New Ways Ministries. (See "Reference Materials" at the end of this book.)

Science continues to give a great deal of updated information about humanity and the cosmos in which we live. Those who choose to examine this new information can make adjustments in their thought process and also live a richer, fuller life. On the other hand, those who choose not to accept new scientific information will limit their understanding and their lives.

Prejudice is one example of what happens when individuals refuse to change their thought process. In the past, ignorant people made the assumption that people of color are inferior to white people. This thought process created slavery, injustice, murder, and war. Those who changed their perception to see all human beings as equals developed new friendships, generated love, enriched their lives, and are helping to reach the goal of world peace.

Principle 2, You can change yourself – you cannot change others is essential for everyone as we move into the future. Change is happening more quickly now than it has ever happened in the history of humankind. As we are confronted with new information about everything in the universe, we have the choice to change, to go with the flow, and to do what is necessary to do what is necessary to create a global village of love and peace. What choice will you make?

G. Application

1. Be the Change You Want to See in Others!

In the Patriarchal Model, leadership imposes or legislates change. This approach, of course, is the application of the "power over" principle. This approach may seem efficient, but it is not always effective.

When I first began to teach at the high school level, I, as well as other young inexperienced teachers, was told to "lay down the law!" "Let the students know from the moment you walk into the room who is the boss!" It was the patriarchal model in all its glory.

Not knowing any better, I followed these directives and ruled with an iron hand. I acted as if I were in armor and made sure the students could not see the human person inside me. This approach was absolutely contrary to my sensitive nature, but I thought, "The experts know more than I do," and felt I had to perform that way. If one of the students was misbehaving, I would point them out publicly, correct them, and at times embarrass, even demean, them. I found out very quickly that these students were creative in finding ways by which they could "get even." Some of these youngsters secretly got to recordings we used in class and damaged them, so that they could no longer be used. Others created cartoons that made me look stupid and circulated them throughout the school. Still others would shout obscenities from the protection of a crowd. It became painfully clear to me, that making life difficult for the students was also making life more difficult for me.

I began to ask myself how I could change my thinking and my actions to achieve a positive relationship with my students. When I came across the application *Be the change you want to see in others,* it was as if a light went on. I began to think, "If I want the students to respect me, I have to respect them. If

I want them to be kind and considerate, I have to be kind and considerate."

I learned how to get rid of my armor and take the risk of being vulnerable. I created a rule: Praise always in public – correct only in private. I began to pay attention to the students who were acting properly in class and commented on that behavior in the classroom. I forced myself to pay attention to the "good" students. If someone was misbehaving, I would work my way to that student as I moved through the classroom, and when another student was speaking, I would simply whisper into his ear: "If you don't behave, I will have to ask you to leave the classroom." Then I would look directly into his eyes and say: "Do you understand?" Then I gave him a broad smile! Most of the time this technique worked. If the student persisted, I had the perfect solution. Without saying a word, I would motion for the student to come with me outside the classroom, where I would put him into a sound-proof rehearsal room, lock the door, and go back into the classroom. When this type of student realized that they had no audience in the rehearsal room, and would not get recognition for misbehavior in the classroom, they changed their behavior.

Another thing I did was to change the structure of the class. Traditional classrooms are typical patriarchal structures: the teacher is in front, sometimes on a platform to make sure he or she is physically above the students (which reinforces the idea of "power over" others). Also in a patriarchal setting, students are sent to a classroom and, in fact, are being told, "You are now ready to study General Music!" Sometimes, however, the students are not in a proper mental place to study that particular subject, at that particular time.

I discovered a method called Individualized Instruction. In this system, the students receive individual packets and are allowed to work through the material on their own. Once they complete a packet, they approach the teacher on a one-to-one basis to be examined on that particular material. They are then given the next packet, and they can then go back to work again. This system allows for flexibility and for individual differences.

It took a long time for me to create this system, but when it was in place, virtually all of my discipline problems disappeared.

Applying *Principle 1, There is beauty in everyone and in everything,* I saw the original, challenging attitude of the students as the factor that motivated me to apply *Principle 2, You Can Change Yourself – You Cannot Change Others.* I then began to change my approach to education. These changes helped me use my creative imagination to produce an innovative methodology that became beneficial for me, for my students, and for other music educators who began to use some of these techniques in their own classrooms.

2. You Don't Have to Be "Right"

I think that Principle 2 can be used effectively when the other person has a need to be "right". Just last night, after I completed a lecture, a couple approached me to ask questions. It took only a few statements from the woman to realize that she believed that I was "New Age" and that she was going to correct me on several things that I had said. I could feel anger beginning to bubble up inside me. First of all, this lady could not define "New Age" but she knew that it was "bad"! It was obvious to me that she had an approach to "truth" that was "right" because she could back it up by authority. My experience has taught me that people like this are looking for security in their lives, and in their belief structures. For that reason, they seem to feel a need to look for people who are not conforming to their "truth," and want to anchor themselves in their own beliefs by convincing, sometimes demanding, others to believe as they do.

With these ideas in the back of my head, I put myself in the shoes of this lovely lady and listened to what she had to say. I fed back to her some of the things she was saying to me: "You mean that you know you have the truth?" "You are afraid that I am teaching New Age to these people?" "You believe that what I am saying is contrary to the Scriptures?" All I tried to do was to help her understand where she was in her thinking. I knew her logic and/or her beliefs were not going to change my beliefs, and I was not going to try converting her to believe the way I do. I think some of the questions I asked let her know that I was listening attentively, and that I was not trying to "push" her anywhere. When she and her friend parted from me, I got the sense that she was satisfied, because she mentioned that she would return the next night to hear more. I felt good about the fact that I was able to allow her to be where she was – and I hoped that she would allow me to be where I am. I do try to be the change I want to see in others.

I know what it is like to be in the place of being "right"! I was there when I was trying to convince my dad that he was wrong as a Jehovah's Witness, and that I was right about the truth I found to be complete in the Catholic Church. The problem with this approach, as I quickly found out, was that in my enthusiasm for being "right," I fractured a very important love relationship. In theory, I knew that the most important teaching of Jesus and the Catholic Church is *love*. In fact, that is the only law! However, I was so busy being "right" that I broke the most important law, the law of love!

The purpose of the principles in this book is to help those who read these pages to put more love into their own lives, and to help others to generate love in their lives. One way to do that is to apply Principle 2 by knowing what you believe and knowing who you are – then by helping others to know what they believe and who they are. This principle and its application can help anyone generate love and create an atmosphere of peace!

3. Choose Someone with Whom You Want to Build or Improve a Relationship; Do to Them or for Them, What You Would Like for Them to Do to You or for You

At one point in my life, I was living with a few Friars who knew little or nothing about what I was doing. Their knowledge about my work came from third parties, most of which was inaccurate or even false. In any case, I wanted the friars to know firsthand what I was doing. I have strong beliefs about the value of my work, not only for individuals who are interested in personal growth and development, but also for all of humanity, which is presently in the process of massive change.

Applying the suggestion above, *Do to or for someone what you would like them to do to or for you,* I decided to take the time and make the effort to move into the areas of work in which the Friars were involved. I first attended a meeting of concerned clergy who were supporting living wage for poor people who had jobs cleaning corporate buildings. At this meeting, I saw Tom in an environment where he was highly respected by those in the group. He had been working in this area for years and obviously was effective in what he was doing. At this meeting, the participants were asking for volunteers to make visits to corporate offices in the city, to speak to people in authority about living wages for janitors and cleaning personnel. It was an opportunity for me to get still more information about this ministry, so I volunteered, and some time later, went to several offices with a nun who had experience in this activity. It was a very rewarding experience.

At a later date, the group had planned a demonstration on the street in front of one of the buildings in the downtown area. Tom was in charge, and I joined the group to add that experience to my repertoire. It too, was rewarding and insightful. I also attended prayer meetings and other gatherings. After a year of these new experiences, I had much more information about Tom's ministry and came to love and respect him far more than I did previously.

I don't know if Tom has any interest in finding out about what I am doing, but it doesn't really make any difference to me. My experiences in his line of work and mission were very rewarding and enriching, but they also have helped me build a better relationship with Tom.

4. Further Applications

a. Help someone with his/her work.

b. Take time out to have fun with someone.

c. Listen to someone who needs to talk.

d. Send a card or e-mail to someone who may need it.

PRINCIPLE 3

You Can Take Control of Your Life

A major topic that has been part of all my teaching is *free will*. We all possess this gift, but with it comes responsibility. When I was a child, my dad told me over and over again, "Buddy, you have to make your own decisions in life, but you also have to pick up the responsibility of those decisions!" That directive has been with me always and has helped me to understand the principle of this chapter.

When I made the decision to enter the Franciscan Order, I did not know all the challenges that would be associated with that choice. When any of us make a life commitment, whether that is a marriage or a profession, we are all taking a risk.

When I entered the Order, the structures were still Medieval. We could bring only a specified amount of clothing, no electronic equipment of any kind: no razor, radio, recorder, etc. Our schedule was something I had only heard about or seen in the movies. We went to bed at 9 p.m. but were awakened at 11:45 p.m. so that at midnight we could chant the Divine Office (the official liturgical prayer of the Church). We chanted the Psalms and listened to readings from the Old and New Testaments as well as writings of the saints. After one hour with the Divine Office, we meditated for one-half hour.

At 1:30 a.m., we were allowed to go to sleep but we were awakened again at 5 a.m. Back we went to the chapel to chant Morning Prayer and to attend the Mass.

We were allowed three meals a day but no food between meals. We showered once a week, received two changes of underclothing each week, and had our outer habit (brown, woolen robe) washed twice a year. We had to wear the habit all the time, even when we worked in the garden or played tennis.

We fasted from November 1 until December 25 and again for 40 days during Lent. If we got permission from our Spiritual Director, we could do a third 40-day fast during the summer in preparation for the feast of St. Michael the Archangel. Needless to say, I had no problem keeping my weight down!

This kind of schedule, and much more, created a challenging lifestyle, but I knew that I had to go through it, because I made a commitment to be a Franciscan Priest. After the 10 years of training, I understood well the challenge of taking responsibility for the decision I made!

In *Success: Full Living,* I spoke directly about the power of choice. The major thrust of that book is this: If you choose goals that are appropriate for you, and/or develop positive attitudes, you will motivate yourself to act in a way in which you will be successful in creating a *satisfying* life. On the other hand, if you choose goals that are not appropriate for you, and/or if you develop negative attitudes, you will motivate yourself to act in a way in which you will create a *dissatisfying* life. I refer to this process as the "Life Mechanism" which is operating every minute of every day in the lives of all human beings. It is because we can make choices that we can take control of our lives.

Stated in a slightly different way, the principle says that *we create our own reality.* The professionals in the field of quantum physics are validating this statement from a scientific point of view. They tell us that *at the quantum level,* the world we know with our senses shifts, and a completely different reality emerges. For example, our senses tell us that wood is solid, and we experience it as solid. However, at the quantum level, the reality of wood is 99.999999 percent space, and what is left are particles that are in constant motion. Our senses tell us that trees are green, but green is only a vibrational frequency which, when picked up by the brain (through the eye), gives us the experience of green. Green exists only in our brains and minds. We experience people as individuals separated from one another. However, at the quantum level, all reality is similar to the night sky (billions of tiny particles where nothing is solid and all of these specks of reality are constantly blinking in and out of existence). We point to a group of stars in the sky and say "Gemini" or "Andromeda," but those realities exist only in our minds! At the quantum level, where there are only vibrational frequencies; there is no distinction between what we call this human being and that human being; there is only one reality! Because of these new scientific insights, we now know that human beings are like the cells in our bodies; all are connected by Cosmic Intelligence, all are One Reality.

Quantum theory goes on to explain that since the Big Bang 13.7 billion years ago, Cosmic Intelligence has been at work creating stars and galaxies, including our sun and the system of plants that surround it. Life emerged on our planet, but only in the last 10,000 years has life taken the form of *Homo sapiens* (humans knowing). At this point in history, we now know that we are the universe reflecting on itself! We are Cosmic Intelligence, knowing that we know, and having the ability to direct and control this faculty of knowing. In fact, we are part of the Creative Energy!

In the world of quantum reality, there is no such thing as a vacuum. Every cubic inch of the universe is filled with an "infinite sea of potentiality". Before *Homo sapiens*, everything in the universe was created by the Intelligence of the cosmos. By dipping into this infinite sea of potentiality, Intelligence created what we experience as the universe. Since the advent of *Homo sapiens*, we human beings, because we are one with this Cosmic Intelligence, have become co-creators of the universe. We, too, can dip into the infinite sea of potentiality and create. In fact, we created the social systems on the planet that we call nations and cultures. All across the planet, we have directed Cosmic Intelligence to create the communication systems that we use daily, the transportation systems that carry us around the globe and into space; we have created religious, philosophical, medical, and political systems that organize our species and an infrastructure that gives us comfort and security.

Please note: Thoughts create reality, but *we choose* what we think about and therefore choose what we create. In the past, we have chosen to have thoughts that created the problems we have today, like climate change, racial discrimination, war, famine, financial crisis, etc. Now, because we are changing our thoughts, our reality is changing. We are working to create clean and environmentally friendly forms of energy, we are choosing to simplify our lives (to live with what we need and not with what we want), we are choosing to look at our planet as a global village, creating systems to help all people live in peace and, at the same time, respect and value our diversity.

At present, I understand the *possible* to be *whatever the mind of a human being can conceive and believe.* My experience is that I create my own future. As I see it, the question *you* need to ask yourself is whether you will create a satisfying future, or a dissatisfying future. Will you choose to think in a positive direction and/or choose goals that are appropriate for you? Your future is always in *your* hands!

A. Nick Vujicic

Nick Vujicic was born on the fourth of December, 1982, in Melbourne, Australia, without limbs – no arms, no legs. Nick was blessed to have parents who had a strong faith in themselves, in life, and in God. They helped Nick to develop positive attitudes about his situation and about life. When he went to school, he was not allowed to go to mainstream schools because the law did not allow disabled students to be with "normal" children. Mrs. Vujicic saw this law as unjust and fought until she was able to get it changed. She wanted her son to integrate himself into society like anyone else.

Even though Nick eventually was allowed to be in public schools, he became discouraged because the children rejected him as weird and bullied him because of his physical differences. Again his parents helped him to develop positive attitudes, suggested that he approach fellow students and start making friends. As Nick became better known to the students he befriended, they began to realize that Nick was just like them, and his friends grew more numerous.

In his teens, he realized that he had valuable speaking ability. He began to look for opportunities to speak to others with challenging life situations and became very effective as an inspirational speaker. With a strong faith in God, he completed a Bachelor of Commerce with a major in financial planning and accounting. He is a professional motivational speaker who carries his powerful message not only to students, but also to corporate professionals and the general public. He continues to set goals like writing books (one titled *No Arms, No Legs, No Worries*) and to be financially independent by the age of 25.

Nick's parents understood *Principle 1, There is beauty in everyone and everything,* as well as *Principle 2, You can change yourself – you cannot change others."*

I viewed a three-minute YouTube presentation of Nick speaking to grade school students and was moved to tears by his faith and his positive attitude. He has an exceptional sense of humor and a captivating personality. What a wonderful example of someone who knows how to apply *Principle 3, You can take control of your life!* (See Nick's book *Life Without Limbs to Life Without Limits.)*

Many medical professionals are making choices that are moving the entire field into the Matriarchal Model. There are more and more doctors who are open to the quantum and holographic models of the universe. This shift in thought is opening new avenues of healing that are noninvasive and nontoxic. As a result, patients are choosing to use these alternative methods of healing, rather than what has been traditional. Just the other day I watched *Bill Moyers' Journal* on PBS. Bill was interviewing a medical doctor from the States who is in the Far East studying Chinese medicine. Other physicians and health care professionals are working with homeopathic remedies; still others are using electro-acupressure, the Rife machine (Wellness Pro Electrotherapy), meditation, etc. All of the above is simply a sign that the entire medical field understands *Principle 3, You can take control of your life!*

B. Sally

Some time ago, we had a nurse who volunteered for the Hermitage, her name was Sally. She began to experience symptoms that led her to believe that she had a tumor on her kidney. She went to her doctor who also believe that the symptoms pointed to a tumor and scheduled her for an MRI. The test confirmed the diagnosis, and the doctor scheduled an operation.

As soon as Sally heard that she would have to have surgery, she came to the Hermitage. It happened to be a Wednesday, when our Energy Circle (meditation support group) meets, and Sally asked if she could have the Energy Circle do a healing meditation for her.

That evening, we had Sally in the center of the circle and asked her to lead the meditation since, as a professional, she knew the biology very well and could best help us in the visualization process. During that meditation, Sally had us visualize the tumor on her kidney being a balloon into which we put a tiny hole. Then she asked us to see the balloon getting smaller and smaller until finally it disappeared. We then, in our minds, pictured Sally in perfect health. The meditation took only five or ten minutes, and afterwards we gave Sally hugs, always sending her our love and our healing.

When it came time for Sally to go to the hospital for surgery, she was feeling much different. She told the doctor that she was sure that the tumor was smaller, or even gone, because the symptoms had disappeared. Sally went so far as to request that the doctor schedule another MRI. The doctor, however, said that these kinds of tumors are malignant 90 percent of the time, and he felt there was no time for another MRI.

When the doctor opened Sally's body, he could find no sign of a tumor, even though a tumor clearly showed in the MRI. He then did an exploratory surgery up her back, thinking that the tumor must be somewhere. He found absolutely nothing, closed the incision and wrote up his report.

Each day after the operation, the doctor stopped into Sally's room to see how she was doing but did not spend time with her. After the third day, Sally insisted that the doctor give her a report on the operation. Sally was not surprised about the outcome. The doctor, on the other hand, was afraid that Sally was about to sue for malpractice and was trying to avoid the issue. (Of course, Sally was not into the mindset of a lawsuit; she just wanted the details.)

Sally never told the doctor about the meditation experience with the people of our Energy Circle because he didn't believe in that "stuff." However, Sally believed in meditation, and that belief proved to be of great advantage to her! Sally was willing to take control of her life, as she believed she could, and was able to find a way to rid herself of cancer.

I, too, am applying Principle 3 in my own life. I go to a traditional doctor because I have to send an annual report to our Provincial Office. I do not take medications or prescription drugs. However, I do see an electro-acupuncturist annually, who helps me with homeopathic remedies. I also have friends and family who are professionals in alternative approaches to healing. These individuals help me choose appropriate food supplement, herbs, and vitamins. I practice meditation and do physical exercise daily as part of my wellness program. My purpose is to take control of my health in as natural and as holistic a way as I can. *Principle 3, You can take control of your life* is an important part of my life!

C. Patrick Henry Hughes

The following story was sent to me by my nephew. It is about a young man named Patrick Henry Hughes. When he sits at a piano and plays, the music filling the air is so beautiful, anyone hearing it knows he is a true master. Then, his voice starts in: "Clair de Lune . . . it means the light of the moon." When Patrick plays, the music speaks of possibility and produces the sounds of promise. The camera moves in a little closer, and then you realize something very special about Patrick that makes the music even sweeter. He does not have eyes. He was born with this condition as well as a painful joint disorder that does not allow him to straighten out his limbs. Walking for him is impossible.

When Patrick's father was interviewed, he said both he and his wife were devastated at the birth of their son. They were asking, "Why us? We worked hard and played by all the rules. We just don't understand." However, their heartbreak ended.

Before Patrick was a year old, his parents sat him down at the piano. That's when the magic started. When either Mom or Dad struck a note, Patrick could find the note on his first or second try. If you don't think that is a gift, try doing that blindfolded!

By age two, Patrick was playing requests like *Twinkle, Twinkle Little Star* and *You Are My Sunshine*. Patrick's dad immediately "got it" and knew what the future might hold. He said: "Okay, we're not going to play baseball; we're going to play music together. Let's see how far we can run with this."

As Patrick grew, his musical ability went through the roof. He performed in middle school and high school and became well-known for his unbelievable gift. When he enrolled at Louisville University, the associate director of bands, Dr. Greg Gyne, asked him to join the marching band.

Patrick's response was, "Yeah right!" He could not imagine a blind man in a wheelchair as part of a marching band.

Enter Wonder Dad! Patrick's father found a way. He joined the marching band with Patrick. No, he doesn't play an instrument, but he goes to every class with Patrick and to every band practice. While Patrick plays the trumpet, his father wheels him around with the rest of the marching band!

His father works the graveyard shift at UPS so that he can spend the day with his son. When asked about his father's workday, Patrick said, "Poor thing. He goes to work about 11 p.m. Monday through Thursday night, gets home about 6 a.m., goes to bed, and sleeps till around 11."

Patrick's dad responded,: "He's my hero. I tell him that. What he goes through has taught me that I don't really have any complaints. I guess a father couldn't ask for anything more than the relationship I have with Patrick."

Patrick said, "God made me blind and unable to walk. Big deal! He gave me musical gifts. I have the great opportunity to meet new people."

This family, too, knows how to apply **You can take control of your life!**

If you would like to hear more about this story and see Patrick and his father in action, you can watch them on YouTube. Just type in "Patrick Henry Hughes."

D. Application

1. Consciously Create Your Own Reality
(Jonathan)

The following is a letter I received from the mother of a young man in Australia who is very busy creating his own reality.

Dear Fr. Justin,

I just wanted to thank you for the absolutely wonderful restorative experience I had after attending just two days of your renewal at St. Thomas More Church.

When I attended the 11 a.m. Sunday Mass I was not aware of the impending renewal. However, once I heard you speak I knew there was no way I could miss the renewal for the rest of the week.

I tried to get my 15-year-old son to attend, but he made an excuse and plunked himself in front of the Play Station (PS2) instead. However, after he heard me gushing about the Sunday night session, he decided to come along with me on Monday. He was absolutely "blown away" too. He wanted to meet you and shake your hand and just keep talking to you via e-mail if that was acceptable. That's why I managed to share with you outside the church and get a calling card from you.

You see, there is something I wish to share with you and ask for your assistance in making my son whole again (physically, mentally, and spiritually).

Jonathan suffered an acute neurological event on the second of January, 2002, when he was only 10 years old and was diagnosed with Moya Moya (a disease caused by blocked arteries at the base of the brain in the area of the basal ganglia). Symptoms can be strokes and resulting disabilities (depending on the affected area of the brain).

At this time, Jonathan suffered the loss of his

ability to speak and also suffered paralysis of the right side.

He was unable to communicate for about three days. Then gradually he was able to articulate single words like "yes" and "no". At this point, we were afraid that he had lost his short and/or long term memory since he was not able to recall who he was or where he was.

It was obvious that this child was petrified because he had no idea what was happening to him. Additionally, he had no way of communicating to us what or how he was feeling. He was such a brave boy throughout it all. He cooperated with the specialists, anesthetists, neurologists, and the neurosurgeon with the endurance and courage of an adult.

The doctors were unable to identify the problem until a range of tests was conducted (CT scans, MRI, MRA, and cerebral angiogram). These were extremely scary from a child's point of view. For the MRI and MRA he had to be encased in tunnel for over half an hour and had to lie completely motionless while the machine pounded and hammered away around his head while taking images of his brain. This was a traumatic experience for him, especially when he woke up from the anesthetic with six strangers holding him down (he could not be permitted to move for fear of an artery hemorrhaging). Though he was distraught and in pain, he conducted himself with unbelievable fortitude and strength.

Then came the day for the dreaded four-and-a-half-hour neurosurgery. Contrary to what we expected, Jonathan was brave and composed despite the fact that he was scared. He had accepted his predicament with the understanding and maturity of someone much older. He simply trusted in us and in the neurosurgeon's ability. He had figured that if this is what we had decided, this was the best option for him.

And it has all paid off. He has since made a

remarkablerecovery.Hehadextensivephysiotherapy, occupational therapy, and speech pathology to assist him regain his full physical strength of the right side, fine motor skills, and verbalization. But it was his indomitable spirit, positive attitude, and sheer determination to be whole again that has brought him through this ordeal. He has been stable since and functions normally. He is in grade 10 now and has his first school examination in three weeks.

On June 15, five years after his first episode, he was diagnosed with Type 1 Diabetes. This has been a major life-altering setback for him He now has to inject himself with insulin four times a day and take at least four blood glucose tests a day.

Despite all of the challenges, Jonathan is a remarkably resilient, happy, and intelligent young lad (yes, I am terribly biased in his favor), and he has been blessed with faith, courage, and fortitude way beyond his years. He has the lofty goal and the ambition to become a neurosurgeon or a pediatric neurologist, and I will to do everything I can to help him achieve that goal.

Jonathan and His Mom
Here is an example of a whole family who is thinking

creatively, but I must add: Jonathan, and many other young people like him, continue to inspire me. These are youngsters who at very young ages, know and use the principles about which I am writing in this book.

Thinking creatively also means being open to new options and ideas. One of my students who is a medical doctor is well aware of the "drug society" we live in and avoids prescribing drugs whenever he can. When he developed high blood pressure, he began to use the relaxation and meditative techniques we teach here at the Hermitage. In only a couple of weeks, he was able to lower his blood pressure without using any drugs. Now when he has patients who have the same challenge, he recommends the recorded meditations that the Hermitage offers before he prescribes a drug.

A study released by an American Heart Association conference in September of 2008, found that even elderly patients who listen to a Mozart sonata or the slow movements of his symphonies for 10 to 15 minutes three times a week can lower their blood pressure and heart rates significantly. Sounds of the ocean can also facilitate physical relaxation that can have the same results. These techniques are not new! They have been used for years to control chronic pain in cancer patients.

The Wellness Pro (electrotherapy) machine and homeopathic remedies are also alternative and nontoxic means for controlling pain and promoting healing and health. (See "Reference Materials" at the end of this volume for further information.)

2. Set Specific Goals
(Lewis Lawes)

Another way of applying *Principle 3, You Can Take Control of Your Life* is by setting specific goals.

When I am teaching the Silva Life System, the very first concept that we work with is this: Your mind creates your reality. In practice, that means discipline of the thought process! Positive thoughts create positive life experience; limiting thoughts create limiting life experience.

Lewis Lawes was only 37 years old when he took over as

warden of Sing Sing prison. That position had the reputation of being a "warden's graveyard" because it was so difficult. In a 12-year period, 10 people held the position, some for only a few months.

Lawes was a man of faith, in himself, in all of humanity, and in God. He had a goal of making this prison of punishment into an institution of rehabilitation. He believed that the job of all penal institutions is to create an environment in which offenders could get involved in personal growth and development. In his own words: "In numerous instances, the crime committed by the member of society is but the natural result of the environment in which the offender was brought up. It may be a case of total illiteracy and ignorance, of a childhood spent in the slums, reared in crowded filthy tenements which make modesty, physical and moral cleanliness, unknown. Should the product of an environment like that be held solely responsible?" With this kind of mental attitude, Lawes began by letting the prisoners know that he believed in them, no matter what their crime. He referred to them as "the boys" and believed that if they were given the opportunity they would choose to become law-abiding citizens. His trust in these men became visible by his actions. For example, every morning he allowed a prisoner, who was convicted of slitting someone's throat, to shave him.

Lawes made himself available 24 hours a day, listening when someone needed to talk, caring when anyone had family difficulties, and doing whatever he could to make life not just bearable, but meaningful and even enjoyable. At one point, the New York Yankees were invited to play ball with the prison team – an event that attracted the attention of the general public and which brought a capacity crowd into this maximum security facility in Ossining, New York. Other events brought famous actors, executives, speakers, and entertainers to the prisoner. Eventually, he created gardens, brought in opera performances, and offered educational programs and team sports. So successful was he with his men, he was able to say, "If I should ever need a man upon whose courage I would rely in the face of gravest danger, I know of hundreds of men, prisoners and ex-prisoners, upon whom I would stake my life."

The prison system that Lawes created was so effective

that when other facilities were exploding with riots, Sing Sing remained calm. When Lawes had to face his first experience of execution, he was very disturbed. First, he went to the Chaplain, who had years of experience with these situations. After listening to the Warden, the Chaplain told him not to worry, that the prisoner had made his peace with God and was ready to accept death. Still not satisfied, Lawes went to the cell of the condemned man to speak to him personally. The prisoner stood up and politely asked, "What can I do for you, mister?"

Upon realizing that it was the Warden and noticing the troubled look on his face, the prisoner assured Lawes that he was sorry for his crime, admitted to his guilt, and believed that God had forgiven him. He then said, "I have a reservation in heaven and I am eager to keep my appointment."

Lawes' wife, Katherine, was also involved in the idealism and commitment of her husband. Both had the same goal in mind, rehabilitation. Katherine was cautioned by others to keep herself and her children distanced from the prisoners. She absolutely refused this advice, and when invited to a basketball game at the prison, she and her family sat with the inmates. She went out of her way to befriend as many of the offenders as she could and helped in exceptional ways. One of the prisoners was blind, and she personally taught him Braille so that he could read. For another who was deaf, she arranged for a teacher to teach sign language. She became like a surrogate mother to them.

She was killed in an automobile accident, and news of her death spread throughout the prison. When gathering on the prison grounds, some of these men were in tears. Her body was made available for viewing at the Lawes' home, about three quarters of a mile from the prison. The prisoners requested the privilege of going to the home to pay their respects, and Lawes allowed them to leave with this simple injunction: "Just be sure you check back in." The gate to the prison was opened, and a long line of inmates, without the supervision of any guards, walked to the home. Everyone checked back into the prison at the end of the day.

When the inmates held their own memorial for Katherine, one of the prisoners spoke for all of them: "To say we loved her seems so pitifully inadequate. To those of us who cannot remember our mothers she was the personification of what we would have liked our mothers to be. To those who have never known the joys of married life, she embodied every wifely virtue and trait we would have longed for in our helpmates. Those of us who have daughters cannot conceive for them a greater destiny than to grow up to resemble Mrs. Lawes in even a few of those characteristics which made her the ideal of everything that is fine and noble in womanhood."

Among the many books that Lawes wrote, his first, *Man's Judgment of Death* is a direct attack on capital punishment, which he did not see as an effective deterrent. His most famous autobiographical book is titled *Twenty Thousand Years in Sing Sing* (the title indicating the total number of years served by prisoners during his leadership). This volume was selected by the Book of the Month Club and became his most influential. *Time* magazine recognized him and his outstanding work by putting his picture on the front cover of one of its issues.

Imagine what would happen if prison administrators today had the same goal! My hope is that some young readers may be inspired by the goals of Lewis Lawes, and prepare themselves for this kind of leadership in penal institutions around the country and around the world!

3. Think Creatively about the Future

Because I knew what my life's vocation was going to be at a very early age, I had a clear goal that would take almost 20 years to reach. My goal was to be a Franciscan Priest, and in my early years of grade school, I knew that I would have to attend a high-school that could prepare me in liberal arts for college.

Being a right-brained person did not make the left-brained academic studies of high-school easy. In fact, as I stated earlier, I had to take the entrance examination for Creighton Prep twice. I clearly remember my first encounters with Latin and considered it nothing more than another academic exercise. It never dawned on me that Latin was supposed to be a medium of communication.

In my third year of high-school I chose to take Greek,

because I knew that it was valuable for my future studies in the seminary. However, after six weeks, the professor approached me with the suggestion, "Bud, I think you should transfer to a Spanish class!"

When I finally got into the seminary, we had to major in philosophy. I would never have chosen this major on my own, but in those days we had no choice. I remember well, the first class in epistemology. We were told to close our eyes and to image a white wall. That was easy enough, but then the professor told us that the purpose of the course was to find out if the white wall really existed or not! I couldn't imagine what the value of this course might be! Not only did I find the courses irrelevant but everything had to be in Latin – lectures, textbooks, discussion, exams, etc. Language was one of my weakest academic areas, so the challenges I faced seemed enormous!

At the end of the first-quarter grading period, I was called into the dean's office. Very sternly, he said, "Justin, there is some doubt about whether you should be here!" He , of course, was referring to my poor grades. He then began to lecture me on how I needed to discipline myself, create systems so that I could improve, etc. As he was lecturing, the thought of leaving the seminary didn't even enter my mind. I knew that I had to become a Franciscan Priest, and this system was the only route to that goal.

When I left the office that day, I began to create a tutoring system for myself. I asked one of my classmates to help me with Latin, another agreed to help me with metaphysics, and others were helping me with psychology, cosmology, etc. To this day, I do not know how I made it through all those years of study but I did. My secret - I kept my goal in mind every day. That image motivated to do whatever was necessary to reach that goal!

Working my way through those years of study had invaluable side effects. I learned to discipline myself, and that habit has been a great asset throughout my life! At the same time, I became sensitive to others who had learning challenges and as a teacher, later in life, was able to develop understanding and patience with all my students. Perhaps one of the greatest gifts of those years was the fact that I was forced to develop left-brain skills, when by nature I had right-brain skills. I have since become much more balanced in my thinking, more stable as a human being, and more creative in planning my future!

It was not easy for me, but I learned to apply *Principle 3, You can take control of your life,* and I continue to do so today!

4. Goal Setting

1.   Write a goal that you would like to achieve during the coming week.

_____

_____

_____

_____

_____

2.   Write a goal that you would like to achieve during the coming month.

_____

_____

_____

_____

_____

3.   Write a goal that you would like to achieve during the

coming year.

_____

_____

_____

_____

_____

4.   Write one goal that you would like to achieve before
you die (be creative!).

_____

_____

_____

_____

_____

PRINCIPLE
4

Giving Freely Is Always Joyful

In our society, at the present time, usually when we speak of giving, we think immediately of giving material things, but let me say something about gifts that are nonmaterial.

Khalil Gibran, in his poem on giving, says,
> You give but little when you give of your possessions.
> It is when you give of yourself that you truly give.

A. Spiritual Gifts

1. Presence and Time
(Archbishop)

I was in a shopping mall in Parma, Ohio, where I saw a young boy standing in front of a talking Christmas tree. The tree asked him, "What do you want for Christmas?" The youngster answered, "I want my daddy to play with me." The tree responded, "Yes, but what else would you like for Christmas?" and again the little boy said, "I want my daddy to play with me." The tree kept insisting that the child think in terms of some "thing," but the child persisted in asking only for time with his daddy.

I am the first to admit that the world we live in is fast and hectic at times. Many of us are so busy "doing," we don't take time to "be." Some think that they can make up for lack of time with friends and loved ones by giving some "thing." Material gifts can never take the place of nonmaterial gifts like quality time with a loved one, personal sharing, holding the hand of someone who needs comfort, celebrating a birthday, or grieving the death of a loved one.

I was working in Perth, West Australia, when I heard that the Archbishop took the time each week to speak to all of the children in the diocesan school system via closed-circuit TV. Students could ask questions of the Archbishop by means of e-mail.

I wanted to get the entire story, so I made an appointment to visit the Archbishop. When I arrived at the chancery office, the Archbishop was on the sidewalk greeting and conversing with passersby. I introduced myself, and we went inside to his office. I asked about his weekly conversations with the students, and he began to give me further details. A sixth-grader asked him why he moved from the huge building that was across the street from the cathedral into the little one-bedroom, one-bath bungalow next door to the chancery office (which had previously been used by the housekeeper). One of the reasons, he explained, was that he wanted to be closer to his people.

Another reason was that there are many homeless people in the center of the city who cannot find a place to sleep because the law does not allowed sleeping on public property. The bungalow has a veranda, a small yard, and an extra garage, and the Archbishop makes that space available to homeless people every night. However, he told me that it is not always convenient. Sometimes he has to get up in the middle of the night to stop fighting over a particular section of the yard or veranda. A few nights previously, he told me, one of the homeless called him on his cell phone (he gives out his cell number in case people need him) and asked if he could speak to a friend that was sleeping on his veranda. He got up, carried the phone to the person outside, and waited until they had completed their conversation.

Sometimes the Archbishop is asked by homeless individuals to be with them when they go to court or to visit them in prison, and he accommodates them when he can. After visiting at the prison, he always leaves money in the account of the person he has visited so that they have something when they are released.

Having heard some of these stories from the Archbishop himself in his weekly talks with the schoolchildren, the sixth-grader mentioned above was very impressed. When she saw a notice in the local newspaper asking for stories of people who "make a difference," she wrote up the story of the Archbishop and sent it in. The organization sponsoring this event invited the Archbishop to give an invocation at one of its luncheons and, after the meal, presented him with an award, based on the article sent in by the sixth-grader.

For me, this is a wonderful example of an Archbishop and a sixth-grader giving personal presence and time, and of an organization that is working to celebrate the efforts of people who make a difference.

2. Joy
(Jimmy)

My brother Jim was the clown of the family and gave all of us a great deal of joy and a lot of laughs. One day when we were children, Ma left the house to help in my grandmother's grocery store. The last thing she said to us was, "Don't you kids fight!" Well, as healthy youngsters who had differences of opinion, we did have our squabbles. That particular day, I got into an argument with my brother Jack, and in the process of pushing each other around the living room, we knocked over the oval coffee table and broke off part of the decorative side panel. Immediately, the fight ended, and we began to figure how to fit the broken pieces back onto the table. We did get them to fit so that the damage was not visible, but they were just hanging there, not attached in any way.

Later that day, when Ma returned home, she came through the front door and, because we unknowingly had moved the coffee table toward the center of the room, in Ma's pathway to the dining room, she bumped the table, and the broken pieces fell to the floor. Her first response was, "I told you kids not to fight!" She immediately went to the kitchen, where she picked up the fly-swatter (in those days made with wire mesh, edged with rubber – a very effective disciplinary tool!). She came toward us, and we moved to the other side of the kitchen table. She then came around the table, and we ran to the other side, Jimmy first, then me, followed by Jack. Around and around we went until Jimmy pulled up a chair, sat down, and began to laugh. We all followed suit, and even Ma sat down, laughing uncontrollably and trying, but without success, to be serious. Through her laughter came this comment: "This isn't funny!" Then we really began to howl! This is the kind of joy Jimmy brought to us all his life.

Jim was the most musically talented of the family and was in a special space when he was entertaining. My fondest image of him is playing a homemade string bass. He had a galvanized washtub that he turned upside down, and he put a small hole in the center of the base. Then he strung tough heavy string through the hole, with a knot at the end to keep it in place. The opposite end of the string was attached to the top of a broomstick handle. The bottom of the handle had a groove sawed through it, which fit on the lip of the tub. By pulling the broomstick back and forth and plucking on the string, he could tighten and loosen the string so that it sounded different pitches, exactly like a string bass. With one foot on the tub, one hand on the broomstick and the other plucking the string, he made that tub sing, to the delight of everyone in the room. More important were the gyrations of his body, the smile on his face, and the Polish expressions that kept us dancing and singing, often into the night! These gifts of time and talent we still enjoy in our memories!

**Brother Jim Teaching My Cousin Ann to
Play His Homemade Bass**

3. Love

When I was living in Parma, Ohio, I met a family who really understood the value of nonmaterial gifts. At Christmastime, the names of each family member were put into a hat, and everyone drew one name. That way, everyone got one material gift, which was wrapped and put under the tree. However, each family member could give as many nonmaterial gifts as they wished. For example, a teenager gave his father this note as a gift: "Dear Dad: I will shine one pair of your shoes every Saturday morning for one year! Merry Christmas!" A 7-year old gave his mother a card with this gift: "Dear Mom, I will give you a hug and a kiss every morning when I get up and every night before I go to bed!" These gifts lasted for an entire year – and some even became habits for a lifetime!

4. Positive Attitude
(John)

Another way to give the nonmaterial gifts of love, joy, and peace is to create a positive attitude. I got the following example from the Internet; perhaps you received a copy also.

John is the kind of person you love to hate. He is always in a good mood and always has something positive to say. When someone would ask him how he was doing, he would reply, "If I were any better, I would be twins!"

He was a natural motivator. If an employee was having a bad day, John was there telling the employee how to look on the positive side of the situation. Seeing his style really made me curious, so one day I went up to him and asked, "I don't get it! You can't be a positive person all the time. How do you do it?"

He replied, "Each morning I wake up and say to myself, you have two choices today. You can choose to be in a good mood, or you can choose to be in a bad mood. I choose to be in a good mood." Each time something bad happens, I can choose to be a victim, or I can choose to learn from it. I choose to learn from it. Every time someone comes to me complaining, I can choose to accept their complaining, or I can point out the positive side of life. I choose the positive side of life."

"Yeah, right, it's not that easy," I protested.

"Yes, it is," he said. "Life is all about choices. When you cut away all the junk, every situation is a choice. You choose how you react to situations. You choose how people affect your mood. You choose to be in a good mood or a bad mood. It's your choice how you live your life."

I reflected on what he said. Soon thereafter, I left the tower industry to start my own business. We lost touch, but I often thought about him when I made a choice about life instead of reacting to it.

Several years later, I heard that he was involved in a serious accident, falling some 60 feet from a communications tower. After 18 hours of surgery and weeks of intensive care, he was released from the hospital with rods placed in his back. I saw him about six months after the accident. When I asked him how he was, he replied, "If I were any better, I'd be twins! Wanna see my scars?"

I declined to see his wounds, but I did ask him what had gone through his mind as the accident took place.

"The first thing that went through my mind was the well-being of my soon-to-be-born daughter," he replied. "Then, as I lay on the ground, I remembered that I had two choices: I could choose to live, or I could choose to die. I chose to live."

"Weren't you scared? Did you lose consciousness?" I asked.

He continued: "The paramedics were great. They kept telling me I was going to be fine, but when they wheeled me into the ER and I saw the expressions on the faces of the doctors and nurses, I got really scared. In their eyes, I read 'He's a dead man.' I knew I needed to take action."

"What did you do?" I asked.

"Well, there was a big burly nurse shouting questions at me," said John. "She asked if I was allergic to anything. 'Yes,' I replied. The doctors and nurses stopped working as they waited for my reply. I took a deep breath and yelled, 'Gravity!'"

Over their laughter, I told them, "I am choosing to live. Operate on me as if I am alive, not dead!"

He lived, thanks to the skill of his doctors, but also because of his amazing attitude. I learned from him that every day we have the choice to live fully.

This kind of story is a gift that can last a lifetime and can change a person's life forever in a positive way!

Attitude, after all, is everything. As Matthew 6:34 reminds us, "Therefore, do not worry about tomorrow, for tomorrow will worry about itself. Each day has enough trouble of its own." Today is the tomorrow you worried about yesterday. Remember *Principle 3, You can take control of your life!*

B. Material Gifts

I do not mean to imply that there is anything wrong with giving material things. On the contrary, material things can be wonderful symbols of spiritual or nonmaterial gifts. One year I led a group to visit the imperial cities of Europe – Prague, Vienna, and Budapest. When we arrived in Prague, I found out that one group member Oscar had purchased beautiful jackets for the members of his family who were traveling with him. Each jacket was personalized with an embossed name. I, too, received one of these jackets. It is one of the most serviceable jackets that I have ever had, and each time I wear it, it's like putting on Oscar's love and support. That jacket also reminds me to send a fresh prayer of love and thanks to him and all of his family!

Material gifts can also be fun! One year, one of our volunteers gave me a beautiful bust of St. Francis for my birthday. It is my custom to put these gifts on my "gift shelf" so that when I need to give someone a gift I can shop at this shelf. However, I must caution you – it is wise to remember from whom you have received the gift!

At Christmastime, I was looking for a special gift for Marcia, a treasured volunteer, who had been traveling a couple of hours each week to the Hermitage to take care of our financial books. When I saw that bust of St. Francis, I knew it was perfect for her, so I carefully wrapped it, and when we had a gift exchange for the staff and volunteers, I couldn't wait to see Marcia's face when she opened this gift. When she did open the box, her face did light up, and she said, "Justin, this is the bust I gave you for your birthday!" Thinking quickly, I responded: "I know, but I also know that you really like it!" That bust came back to me on my birthday, and the following Christmas it went back to Marcia. Neither of us had to shop for each other on those days for several years!

1. Material Things Can Carry Spiritual Gifts
(Jim Castle)

The following story is, for me, a good illustration of the importance of material gifts.

Jim Castle was tired when he boarded his plane in Cincinnati, Ohio, that night in 1981. The 45-year-old management consultant had put on a weeklong series of business meetings and seminars, and now he sank gratefully into his seat ready for the flight home to Kansas City, Missouri. As more passengers entered, the place hummed with conversation, mixed with the sound of bags being stowed. Then, suddenly, people fell silent. The quiet moved slowly up the aisle like an invisible wake behind a boat. Jim craned his head to see what was happening, and his mouth dropped open. Walking up the aisle were two nuns clad in simple white habits bordered in blue. He recognized the familiar face of one at once, the wrinkled skin, and the eyes warmly intent. This was a face he'd seen in newscasts and on the cover of *Time*. The two nuns halted, and Jim realized that his seat companion was going to be Mother Teresa! As the last few passengers settled in, Mother Teresa and her companion pulled out rosaries. Each decade of the beads was a different color, Jim noticed. The decades represented various areas of the world, Mother Teresa told him later, and added, "I pray for the poor and dying on each continent."

The airplane taxied to the runway, and the two women began to pray, their voices a low murmur. Though Jim considered himself a not very religious Catholic who went to church mostly out of habit, inexplicably he found himself joining in. By the time they murmured the final prayer, the plane had reached cruising altitude. Mother Teresa turned toward him. For the first time in his life, Jim understood what people meant when they spoke of a person possessing an "aura." As she gazed at him, a sense of peace filled him; he could no more see it than he could see the wind, but he felt it, just as surely as he felt a warm summer breeze.

"Young man," she inquired, "do you say the rosary often?" "No, not really," he admitted. She took his hand, while her eyes probed his. Then she smiled. "Well, you will now." And she dropped her rosary into his palm. An hour later, Jim entered the Kansas City airport, where he was met by his wife, Ruth. "What in the world?" Ruth asked when she noticed the rosary in his hand. They kissed, and Jim described his encounter. Driving home, he said. "I feel as if I met a true sister of God." Nine months later, Jim and Ruth visited Connie, a friend of theirs for several years. Connie confessed that she'd been told she had ovarian cancer. "The doctor says it's a tough case," said Connie, "but I'm going to fight it. I won't give up." Jim clasped her hand. Then, after reaching into his pocket, he gently twined Mother Teresa's rosary around her fingers. He told her the story and said, "Keep it with you, Connie. It may help." Although Connie wasn't Catholic, her hand closed willingly around the small plastic beads.

"Thank you," she whispered. "I hope I can return it."

More than a year passed before Jim saw Connie again. This time her face was glowing; she hurried toward him and handed him the rosary. "I carried it with me all year," she said. "I've had surgery and have been on chemotherapy, too. Last month, the doctors did second-look surgery, and the tumor's gone. Completely!" Her eyes met Jim's. "I knew it was time to give the rosary back."

In the fall of 1987, Ruth's sister, Liz, fell into a deep depression after her divorce. She asked Jim if she could borrow the rosary, and when he sent it, she hung it over her bedpost in a small velvet bag. "At night I held on to it, just physically held on. I was so lonely and afraid," she said later, "yet when I gripped that rosary, I felt as if I held a loving hand." Gradually, Liz pulled her life together, and she mailed the rosary back. "Someone else may need it," she said. Then one night in 1988, a stranger telephoned Ruth. She'd heard about the rosary from a neighbor and asked if she could borrow it to take to the hospital, where her mother lay in a coma. The family hoped the rosary might help their mother die peacefully. A few days later, the woman returned the beads. "The nurses told me a coma patient can still hear," she said, "so I explained to my mother that I had Mother Teresa's rosary, and that when I gave it to her she could let go. As soon as I folded her hand around the rosary, we saw her face relax. The lines of her face smoothed out until she looked so peaceful, so young." Holding back tears, the woman continued: "A few minutes later she was gone." Fervently, she gripped Ruth's hands. "Thank you," she whispered.

Is there special power in those humble beads? Is the power of the human spirit simply renewed in each person who borrows the rosary?

Jim knows only that requests continue to come, often unexpectedly. He always lends the rosary with this one request: "When you're through needing it, send it back. Someone else may need it." Jim's own life has changed, too, since his unexpected meeting on the airplane. When he realized Mother Teresa carries everything she owns in a small bag, he made an effort to simplify his own life. "I try to remember what really counts – not money, or titles, or possessions, but the way we love others," he says. Jim now knows from experience about *Principle 4, Giving freely is always joyful!*

You, too, can give healing to others through physical objects. If you have any training in meditation, you know that *anyone* can energize physical objects with healing energy. Simply by holding an object, going into a meditative state, consciously connecting with Universal Intelligence in *your* person, and visualizing healing energy flowing from you to the object, energy will collect in the object. You can then program the object to release this energy whenever anyone comes in contact with the object, either physically or visually.

In the past, we were led to believe that only priests or ministers could bless objects. The fact is, anyone can bless an object and use it as a means of sending love and healing energy to others.

Love, healing, and other spiritual energies are the most valuable gifts we can give to another person. What is so wonderful about giving nonmaterial gifts is the fact that when given, they multiply. For example, the more love you give away, the more there is. If you radiate peace, everywhere you go will become a peaceful place. Please note: *Giving freely is always joyful!*

2. Corporate Giving

a. Hospital Sisters of St. Francis

In 2002 the Hospital Sisters of St. Francis in Springfield, Illinois, founded a unique venture – the Hospital Sisters Mission Outreach. Eight years later the outreach is going strong and meeting with great success. The Mission Outreach is a not-for-profit organization focused on the recovery and responsible redistribution of health care equipment and supplies to developing countries. In addition to collecting medical equipment and supplies from the Hospital Sisters Health System's 13 hospitals, today it gathers items from 20 other hospitals in Illinois and Wisconsin.

The Sisters' approach is unique. Donations are tested, processed, and maintained in an online inventory, which is made available to their domestic and overseas recipients. The Sisters solicit orders from the end-users and customize shipments to their expressed needs. In 2007 Mission Outreach recovered more than 670,000 pounds of usable equipment and supplies that would otherwise have been dumped in landfills. 380,000 pounds of supplies and equipment, valued at $2.4 million, were shipped to 29 countries to include health care institutions in Nigeria, Ukraine, Haiti, Honduras, and Cuba, to mention a few. On average, each shipment contained items totaling $140,000 in value.

The Hospital Sisters of St. Francis are pleased to report that Mission Outreach has been named a "preferred medical partner" of the U.S. Navy's Project Handclasp, which provides transportation aid via U.S. naval vessels. In the Sisters' most recent naval collaborations, medical equipment and supplies were provided to 12 countries in Central and South America and West Africa. These women give for the pure joy of giving. They do not know the individuals who will be healed by their giving, but they continue to give for the satisfaction that makes their lives so rich and meaningful. If you are interested, check the website (www.mission-outreach.org) to keep abreast with what is new at Mission Outreach, and/or if you are in Springfield, Illinois, visit the Sisters to see the operation in action.

b. Holy Spirit of Freedom Community

I happened to be in Perth, Australia, in the downtown area waiting for a ride. A young man and an older woman got out of a car and proceeded to take a large coffee urn out of their trunk (or "boot," as they say in Australia) as well as a basket of cookies ("biscuits"). We struck up a conversation, and they explained that they were members of a community that has a special ministry to the poor, the disadvantaged, and the homeless. Each day, members of their community go to the inner city to be with children who live on the street, as well as with prostitutes and drug addicts. They carry coffee and a bit of food, but their main purpose is to offer love, understanding, and friendship to those who really need it. They know their clientele on a first-name basis, but have no expectations for the future of those they meet. Their purpose is simply to offer them love, friendship, and support. The joy and peace that were shown on the faces of these two people let me know that they were giving freely with no expectation of any kind. Their reward was the joy they experienced in their hearts.

c. Giving Freely

In his poem on giving, Gibran describes a special kind of giving person.

> "There are those who give and know not pain in
> giving nor do they seek joy nor give with
> mindfulness of virtue;
> They give as in yonder valley the myrtle breathes its
> fragrance into space.
> Through the hands of such as these God speaks, and
> from behind their eyes, God smiles upon the
> earth."

3. Giving Understanding

The following is a story about a very kind person who was working in the dead letter office of the U.S. Postal Service, someone we will probably never be able to identify, but someone who has left a lasting impression on a great many people.

Abbey was a dog that died at 14 years of age. The day after her death, Meredith, who was only 4 years old, came to her mother crying and sharing how much she missed Abbey. She asked if she could write a letter to God so that when Abbey got to heaven, God would recognize her. Meredith dictated the letter, and her mother wrote it down.

> Dear God:
> Will you please take care of my dog? She died yesterday and is with you in heaven. I miss her very much. I am happy that you let me have her as my dog even though she got sick. I hope you will play with her. She likes to play with balls and to swim. I am sending a picture of her so when you see her you will know that she is my dog. I really miss her.
>
> Love,
> Meredith

They put the letter into an envelope with a picture of Abbey and Meredith, and addressed it to "God/Heaven." There was, of course, a return address on it, and Meredith pasted several stamps on the front of the envelope because, she said, "It will take lots of stamps to get the letter all the way to heaven." That afternoon Meredith dropped the letter into the letterbox at the post office.

A few days later, Meredith asked her mom if God had gotten the letter yet. Mom told her that she thought He had.

The following day there was a package wrapped in gold paper on the front porch addressed "To Meredith." Meredith opened it and inside was a book by Mister Rogers called *When a Pet Dies.* Taped to the inside front cover of the book was the letter Meredith had dictated and the envelope in which it had been sent. On the opposite page was the picture of Abbey and Meredith along with this note:

Dear Meredith:

Abbey arrived safely in heaven. Having the picture was a big help. I recognized Abbey right away. She isn't sick anymore. Her spirit is here with me just like it stays in your heart. She loved being your dog. Since we don't need our bodies here in heaven, I don't have any pockets to keep your picture in, so I am sending it back to you in this little book for you to keep and have something to remember Abbey by.

Thank you for the beautiful letter and thank your mother for helping you write it and sending it to me. What a wonderful mother you have. I picked her especially for you. I send my blessing every day, and remember that I love you very much. By the way, I am wherever there is love.

Love,
God

The person in the post office who took the time and effort to give such peace to an unknown little girl is a person who really knows the joy in giving freely! *Principle 4: Giving freely is always joyful!*

4. Sharing Life Experience

Father John Powell, a professor at Loyola University in Chicago, wrote the following about a student in his Theology of Faith class named Tommy.

I stood watching my university students file into the classroom for our first session in The Theology of Faith. That was the day that I first saw Tommy. My eyes and my mind both blinked. He was combing his long flaxen hair, which hung six inches below his shoulders. It was the first time I had ever seen a boy with hair that long, but I knew in my mind that it isn't what's *on* your head, but what's *in* it that counts. However, on that day, I was unprepared, and my emotions flipped. I immediately filed Tommy under "S" for strange . . . very strange.

Tommy turned out to be the "atheist in residence" in my Theology of Faith course. He constantly objected to, smirked at, or whined about the possibility of an unconditionally loving Father/God. We lived with each other in relative peace for one semester, although I must admit that he was for me, at times, a serious pain in the back pew!

When he came up at the end of the course to turn in his final exam, he asked in a cynical tone, "Do you think I'll ever find God?"

I decided instantly on a little shock therapy. "No!" I said very emphatically.

"Why not?" he responded. "I thought that was the product you were pushing."

I let him get five steps from the classroom door and then called out, "Tommy! I don't think you'll ever find God, but I am absolutely certain that God will find you!"

He shrugged a little and left my class and my life.

I felt slightly disappointed at the thought that he had missed my clever line – God will find you! At least I thought it was clever.

Later, I heard that Tommy had graduated, and I was duly grateful. Then a sad report came. I heard that Tommy had terminal cancer. Before I could search him out, he came to see me. When he walked into my office, his body was very badly wasted, and the long hair had all fallen out as a result of chemotherapy. But his eyes were bright, and his voice was firm.

"Tommy, I've thought about you so often; I hear you are sick," I blurted out.

"Oh, yes, very sick. I have cancer in both lungs. It's a matter of weeks."

"Can you talk about it, Tom?" I asked.

"Sure, what would you like to know?" he replied.

"What's it like to be only 24 and dying?"

"Well, it could be worse."

"Like what?"

"Well, like being 50 and having no values or ideals, like being 50 and thinking that booze, seducing women, and making money are the real biggies in life."

I began to look through my mental file cabinet under "S" where I had filed Tommy as strange. (It seems as though everybody I try to reject by classification, God sends back into my life to educate me.)

"But what I really came to see you about," Tom said, "is something you said to me on the last day of class." (He remembered!)

He continued: "I asked you if you thought I would ever find God, and you said, 'No!' which surprised me. Then you said, 'But God will find you.' I thought about that a lot, even though my search for God was hardly intense at that time. (My clever line. He thought about that a lot!)

"But when the doctors removed a lump from my groin and told me that it was malignant, that's when I got serious about locating God. And when the malignancy spread into my vital organs, I really began banging bloody fists against the bronze doors of heaven. But God did not come out. In fact, nothing happened. Did you ever try anything for a long time, with great effort, and with no success? You get psychologically glutted, fed up with trying, and then you quit.

"Well, one day I woke up, and instead of throwing a few more futile appeals over that high brick wall to a God who may be or may not be there, I just quit. I decided that I didn't really care about God, about the afterlife, or anything like that. I decided to spend what time I had left doing something more profitable. I thought about you and your class, and I remembered something wise you had said: 'The essential sadness is to go through life without loving. But it would be almost equally sad to go through life and leave this world without ever telling those you loved that you had loved them.'

"So, I began with the hardest one, my dad. He was reading the newspaper when I approached him.

"'Dad.'

"'Yes, what?' he asked without lowering the newspaper.

"'Dad, I would like to talk with you.'

"'Well, talk.'

"'I mean . . . it's really important.'

"The newspaper came down three slow inches. 'What is it?'

"'Dad, I love you. I just wanted you to know that.'"

Tom smiled at me and said it with obvious satisfaction, as though he felt a warm and secret joy flowing inside of him.

"The newspaper fluttered to the floor. Then my father did two things I could never remember him ever doing before. He cried, and he hugged me. We talked all night, even though he had to go to work the next morning. It felt so good to be close to my farther, to see his tears, to feel his hug, to hear him say that he loved me too.

"It was easier with my mother and little brother. They cried with me, too, and we hugged each other, and started saying real nice things to each other. I was only sorry about one thing – that I had waited so long. Here I was, just beginning to open up to all the people I had actually been close to.

"Then one day, I turned around, and God was there. God didn't come to me when I pleaded. I guess I was like an animal trainer holding out a hoop, 'C'mon, jump through. C'mon, I'll give you three days, three weeks.' Apparently God does things in

God's own way and hour. The important thing is that God was there. God found me! You were right. God found me even after I stopped looking for God."

"Tommy," I practically gasped," I think you are saying something very important and much more universal than you realize. To me, at least, you are saying that the surest way to find God is not to make God a private possession, a problem solver, or an instant consolation in time of need, but rather by opening to love. You know, the Apostle John said that. He said, 'God is love, and anyone who lives in love is living with God, and God is living in him.'

"Tom, could I ask you a favor? You know, when I had you in class, you were a real pain. But [laughingly] you can make it all up to me now. Would you come into my present Theology of Faith course and tell them what you have just told me? If I told them the same thing, it wouldn't be half as effective as if you were to tell it."

"Ooh . . . I was ready for you, but I don't know if I'm ready for your class."

"Tom, think about it. If and when you are ready, give me a call."

In a few days Tom called, said he was ready for the class, that he wanted to do that for God and for me. So we scheduled a date. However, he never made it. He had another appointment, far more important than the one with me and my class. Of course, his life was not really ended by his death, only changed. He made the great step from faith into vision. He found a life far more beautiful than the eye of any human had ever seen, or the ear of any human had ever heard, or the mind of any human had ever imagined.

Before he died, we talked one last time. "I'm not going to make it to your class," he said.

"I know, Tom."

"Will you tell them for me? Will you . . . tell the whole world for me?"

"I will, Tom. I'll tell them. I'll do my best."

So, to all of you who have been kind enough to read this simple story about God's love, thank you for listening. And to you, Tommy, somewhere in the sunlit, verdant hills of heaven, I told them, Tommy, as best I could.

If this story means anything to you, please pass it on to a friend or two. It is a true story and is not enhanced for publicity purposes.

> With thanks,
> Rev. John Powell,
> Professor, Loyola University
> Chicago

P.S. "I expect to pass through this world but once. Any good therefore that I can do or any kindness that I can show to any human being, let me do it now. Let me not defer or neglect it, for I shall not pass this way again." [—Stephen Grellet]

All of us have life-experiences that speak about love, joy, peace, healing, and other good things. As children, almost every night during the summer, we would sit on my grandmother's porch after she closed the grocery store. She would send my Mom or one of my aunts or uncles to the corner tavern to get a jug of beer, while she gathered a large bag of potato chips and some cheese from the store. I remember sitting on the floor of the porch, listening to Busia telling her life stories and always being fascinated. She told of her long and challenging journey from Poland to the States, how when she needed help, there was always someone there to help her, and as a result, she learned to help others.

In some ways, my grandmother taught me more by her stories than any professor of theology taught me from books. Those life experiences speak very loudly to those who have the opportunity to hear them!

You have *your* stories. *Principle 4: Giving freely is always joyful.*

5. Learning to Give Freely

Again, in Gibran's poem, there is a description of those who find giving difficult:
"And there are those who give with pain, and that pain is their baptism."

a. Daddy's Story

When we were growing up, we had what we needed and not much more. However, when our parents were living alone after we grew up, Mom had an allowance, and her goal was to give it all away each month. Giving was great fun for her!

When I came home one summer for vacation, she insisted that she pay for my plane fare. I explained that my fare was paid for by the Order, and it wasn't necessary for me to be reimbursed. Her reply was that she gave to my other brothers and their wives throughout the year and wanted to "even the score" when I came home for vacation.

Daddy, on the other hand, had a difficult time giving. He would drive halfway across town to buy butter for a few pennies less. He was the kind of person who saved butter cartons and glass jars because "you never know when you will need them!"

One year, when Ma was about to give me money from her allowance for my airfare, I asked why she took the money out of her allowance when it could come from the family checking account. She thought that was a great idea and asked Daddy to write me a check. Daddy was not happy with this arrangement, but he grudgingly wrote the check.

The following year, Ma was going to ask Daddy to write a check for me, and I asked her if *she* could write the check because Daddy always got so upset. She thought that was a better idea, and as she was writing the check she said, "He can get upset when the bank statement comes!"

After Ma died, Daddy was able to give more easily, and eventually he got to the point where he had no problem giving at all; in fact, giving, for him, came to be joyful!

b. My Story

Some people give and expect something in return. In my estimation, this approach is not a good idea because it can be a set-up for disappointment. The principle states that giving *freely* is always joyful.

Over the years, I have had individuals tell me that I allow people to take advantage of me because I give freely of my time and talent without getting anything in return. My response to these kinds of comments is, "No one takes advantage of me since I find joy in the giving!" If the person to whom I give misuses the gift, that's his or her problem. My satisfaction is in the giving itself!

6. Give Away What You Don't Need (Live Simply!)

Some people, I find, have a very difficult time giving things away. It is as if the things have a hold on them. My question then is, "Are you in charge of the things you have, or are they in charge of you?"

Don Aslett, in his book *Clutter's Last Stand* has some wonderful examples of people who allow "things" to get hold of them. A family moved into a new home and piled all of their excess "stuff" in the several rooms downstairs. They never took the time to go through all of the junk that they brought with them, so it just sat there. After some time, they decided that they wanted to put a fireplace in the downstairs family room and contacted a local mason. When the mason asked for the address, he commented, "I think I put a fireplace in that home two years ago." The family went downstairs and started moving all of the "stuff" they had piled up in the family room. Sure enough, to their amazement, they found a beautiful fireplace!

An elderly woman had lived in her home for 50 years, and because of her age and health challenges, she was being forced to move into an apartment. She told her children that they would have to get rid of all the things she had collected over the years and directed them to keep only the "good stuff." The children backed a 16-foot-long, 2½-ton grain truck to the side of the house and started with the attic. They filled the truck to overflowing and still had not completed the upstairs rooms. One of the sons was a junk collector himself and saved only 20 boxes of "good stuff." It took three truckloads to dispose of the rest of the junk! The mother was thrilled to begin a new life in her dejunked living space.

C. Application

1. As a parent, share with your children
    a. Your first love.
    b. Your first job.
    c. How you met your spouse.
    d. The details of your child's birth.

2. As a child, ask your parents
    a. To share the experience of their first love.
    b. How they met.
    c. How they decided to marry.
    d. The details of your birth.

3. Thank people who serve you well, for example in the supermarket or in a restaurant.

4. Greet people with a smile or, if it is appropriate, ask, "Are you having fun yet?"

5. Give away at least five hugs a day.

6. How many compliments can you give away in a day?

7. Clean out a drawer, closet, or garage. Then pay attention to how you feel afterwards!

8. In meditation, send healing to a plant, a book, a card, etc., and then give it to a person who needs healing.

PRINCIPLE 5

It Is Important for Others to Give to You

After I had given a program in a small town in Indiana, an older woman who volunteered as a traffic coordinator at a local school wrote the following:

Dear Fr. Justin:
I had to share this experience with you. After the Wednesday evening program on *Giving and Allowing others to give to you*, I left the Church in a big hurry to go home and pack for my trip on Thursday. When I started the car, it kind of sputtered, but I didn't think much about it. It died 3 or 4 times within the first block and the last time it died I couldn't get it started again. It was a cold, damp night and the wind was howling. When I got out of the car, I remembered that I had parked up against the school and there was a big pile of snow there. I checked the tail pipe and sure enough, it was packed very tightly with snow and there was no digging it out. It was packed in there very tightly! I got my gloves on but nothing would get that snow out of the pipe.
I saw a car approaching and waved my arms frantically. The car pulled over and two gentlemen got out. I explained my problem and they began to look in their car for something that would dig out the snow. They found a screw driver and were able to remove the snow in no time at all and I was able to be on my way.

Your homework for that night was to 1) ask for help (which I did) and 2) accept it with a gracious thank you (which I did). I am a "giver" and it's hard for me to ask for and accept help for anything – but I did so graciously that night. Talk about learning lessons – and so quick too!

Thank you Fr. Justin!

There are a good many people like the author above, individuals who can give easily but just can't seem to find it easy to receive from others. Do you find it easy to accept what others have to offer?

A. Receiving Service from Others
(Dr. Elisabeth Kubler-Ross)

During a workshop with Dr. Kubler-Ross, author of the famous book *Death and Dying*, she told us this story about her mother.

Her mother was one of those individuals who always had to have the books balanced. If a neighbor gave her a pie on Monday, she returned another pie on Tuesday. She simply could not receive anything graciously without feeling bound to repay the favor.

As she grew older, her health began to fail, and eventually she had to be admitted to a nursing home, where she had to be waited on hand and foot. It was extremely difficult for her to be receiving all of this attention without being able to repay anything.

Dr. Kubler-Ross tried everything she could to help her mother feel comfortable, but nothing seemed to work. Finally, she told her mother, "Mother, perhaps this is the lesson you have to learn before you can be released into eternal life!"

Much later, the mother finally got to the point where she could accept the services of the staff with ease and with a simple but gracious "thank you." Not long after she made this change in her life, she very peacefully slept away into eternal life!

Do you have this kind of challenge in your life? Perhaps this is an area you need to work on. *Principle 5, It is important for others to give to you.*

B. Receiving Physical Gifts

As a Franciscan Friar, I take a promise to live a simple life with few things. I have never had a salary nor a bank account – but neither have I ever seen a state or federal tax form! Early on in my Franciscan career, I remember how difficult it was for me to receive gifts from the people with whom I worked, knowing that I could not return the gifts – at least not material gifts. As a result, I began to find it easy to receive graciously and to be satisfied with sending a personal thank-you or sometimes a poem.

The very first time I sent a poem in the mail, I did so with much fear, thinking that I would be making a fool of myself. Poems are, after all, very personal exposures of one's inner life. Can you imagine how excited I was when I got a phone call from the person to whom I had sent the poem, telling me she was so impressed that she had it framed and put on her living-room wall? That experience not only taught me how to receive easily and graciously, but it also gave me the confidence I needed to continue writing poetry.

C. Receiving Honest Compliments

My experience tells me that many people have a challenge in accepting compliments graciously. In my estimation, the reason for this situation is the person receiving the compliment has a poor self-image. A healthy self-image is a basic and necessary foundation that we all need if we are to be happy and grounded individuals.

I was visiting friends in the Cleveland area, and their 7-year-old son was playing with a puzzle in the form of a three-dimensional cube. We watched as he manipulated the puzzle this way and that, and no matter how the cube was undone, he could get it back to perfect form in just a few minutes. I told the youngster that he was very good at working that puzzle, and he simply responded, "I know!" This child, being transparent, recognized his talent and was able to accept a compliment easily and admit to the talent he had.

As adults we do the same thing when a person offers an honest compliment and we simply answer, "Thank you!" That response is an honest statement that we acknowledge and own the talent or skill, and the "thank you" reinforces a positive self-image. That kind of self-acceptance is valuable grounding material for anyone!

At this writing, I have a friend who is one of the best shoppers I know. She is able to buy things that create wonderful ensembles. Every time I see her in something striking (which is often), I make a point of offering a compliment. More often than not, she responds that she was able to get this jacket at a discount store of some kind, or that this blouse is very old, or some other comment to shy away from simply saying, "Thank you!" The above comments are, in fact, excuses for being talented and creative. They are also a psychological self-"put-down," which can easily get anchored in the person's subconscious and have a lasting negative effect.

We are all unique and valuable people, and we have every right to own up to that reality. Accepting honest compliments for personal characteristics, talents, skills, or accomplishments is a positive experience for the person but also an acknowledgement that the Creator has done a wonderful job!

Accepting honest compliments graciously may seem like a small item, but it is one way to build self-image, to concentrate on the goodness that is present in our lives and in our persons, as well as a means of building positive relationships with other individuals.

All of us can help friends and acquaintances to practice accepting honest compliments by giving them away freely. At one point in my life, I was living with a Friar who often seemed sad, even depressed. I decided to make a point of reflecting the good that I saw in him. He was, at that time, the Guardian of the house in which I was living, and when he would do something for the community, I would thank him for being there for all of us and point to a specific act that reflected that reality. At first, my comments were met with no acknowledgment, but as I continued to give the compliments, I eventually got a simple "Thank you!" I was amazed how this little exercise on my part helped him to develop a more positive self-image, and, at the same time, helped to build our relationship.

Consider creating a habit of accepting honest compliments by simply saying, "Thank you" and perhaps adding the comment "I appreciate that" or, if the situation applies, you can return the compliment by saying, "It takes one to know one!" I can promise you, when you know yourself well and you can easily receive honest compliments, you will realize that you are a much more grounded person and that you are capable of making your self-image better and better!

D. Receiving Ideas and Insights

Children grow and mature because they are open to receive all kinds of new information without asking questions or closing off their minds. Early on, children experience the earth as flat. Then, when they go to school and hear the teacher telling them that the earth is a sphere, they accept it and begin to reshape their mental perception of the world. Children really do have open minds – that's why they learn so quickly.

1. Healing

When I am teaching a meditation class to children and tell them that their mind is connected to, and one with, Universal Mind, or Cosmic Mind, they simply say, "Okay." Once that piece of information is recorded and we begin to apply healing techniques, the learning process becomes very easy. I can tell them, for example, that when they skin a knee, or bump an elbow, and feel pain, all they have to do is brush that part of their body with their hand and mentally say, "Gone," and the pain disappears. Their response is always, "Okay". This kind of subconscious "programming" makes it possible for them to control pain.

Of course this "technique" is nothing new. Even when I was a child and hurt myself, Ma would say, "Buddy, let me kiss it, and it will be all right!" – and the kiss worked. This approach, however, is limiting because it makes the child dependent on the parent even though the same mental mechanism is at work.

When I am teaching meditation to adults, I tell them (as I do the children) that all they have to do to control pain is to relax, go into a meditative state, and then brush a hand over the area of pain and mentally say, "Gone". The response I usually get from adults is a very sarcastic "Sure." The reason for this kind of response is that adults have been "programmed" to believe that pain can be controlled only by a pill. If they close their minds to an approach that is new to them, they are throwing away an opportunity for taking greater control of their lives, as well as creating a technique that can enhance the quality of their lives.

Some adults get so comfortable with beliefs they have held since childhood, they refuse to examine any new idea or alternative. They fight change. In my first book, *Success: Full Living,* I described life as change. Change is happening all the time, and life will continue to change. Those who can go with the flow of this change will have happy, fulfilled lives. Those who fight the change will be forever upset and/or annoyed.

2. Sexual Orientation

The movie *The Bible Tells Me So* is the true story of a mother who had a gay son. Because she came from a very fundamentalist religious background, she believed that being gay was an abomination and of course was able to quote the Bible to support her belief. She did everything she could to change her son, but all she did was to create more stress in the life of a young man who was already stressed out. When her son took his own life, she felt, in part, responsible and began to open her mind to a different viewpoint. She visited a local Metropolitan Community Church to which her son belonged and which exists especially for the gay, lesbian, bisexual, and transgendered community. She began to understand that quotes of the Bible used by her minister were taken out of context. In Leviticus 18:22, it does indeed say that if a man lies with another man, it is an abomination. However, Leviticus 25:44 also says that I may possess slaves, both male and female, provided they are purchased from neighboring nations. Does that mean that here in the United States we can make slaves of Mexicans as well as of Canadians? Exodus 21:7 says that you may sell your daughter. Exodus 35:2 says that no one is to work on the Sabbath, and if they do, they must be put to death.

This mother began to understand that there are experts who can interpret the Bible in the way it was meant to be understood by the people of the day. She began to understand the teaching of unconditional and universal love as taught by Jesus. When she opened her mind to these wonderful gifts from informed and loving people, she was able to forgive herself and is now spending her time helping other parents to accept and love their gay or lesbian children.

When Jesus said, "The truth will set you free," that was no moral platitude; it is a reality. When you open your mind to accept the gift of new insight from others, you accept an opportunity to become a better person, an opportunity to broaden your perspective, and most of all an opportunity to enrich your life!

If you close your mind to new ideas, to new insights, to new horizons, to new life experience, you will be illiterate. The illiterate of this century are not those who cannot read or write – but rather those who refuse to learn, refuse to relearn, or refuse to unlearn what they have acquired in the past. We cannot forget the truth that has been given to us in the past, but we are moving on to truth that is being unveiled for us in every corner of the globe, and which is making our lives more meaningful and exciting! We are all challenged to unlearn some of the things we were taught in school, or by the state, or even by the Church. Those who are open to learning will one day move from the category of *Homo sapiens* ("human knowing"), to the next evolutionary stage of *Homo noeticus* ("human thinking"). Father Ed Hays writes in his *A Book of Wonders*:

> Force me to strenuously use an eraser
> to remove my mind's old knowledge
> that stymies my soul and stagnates me,
> so I'll be eager and ready to learn new ways.

Would that all of us could say this prayer daily and move ourselves, and our world, into a better place.

3. Gender and Other Sexual Issues

In the past, Western Culture taught that sexual orientation is simple: God created heterosexual human beings, and anything else is either wrong or against nature. Given that premise, it is logical to conclude that categories like gay, lesbian, bisexual, or transsexual are aberrations, morally wrong, and against natural law.

But what happens when the basic assumption turns out to be wrong? What happens when we discover that sexual orientation and gender are very diverse? Logically, conclusions drawn from a previous faulty premise are going to be faulty also.

For example, the Catholic Church had taught in the past that the primary purpose of sex and marriage is to generate offspring. This teaching put all the other ends of marriage, like satisfying sexual pleasure, building a loving relationship, stabilizing emotional and psychological health, etc., into a secondary place, sometimes even in a sinful place. In this context, moral language was developed to describe sexual intercourse between married persons as "at most venial sin."

The Second Vatican Council made some major changes in marriage theology and clearly stated that *all* the ends of marriage were of equal importance. This statement has caused a lot of turmoil between the leadership in the Church, professional theologians, and the laity. Changing this one viewpoint also causes the moral and ethical conclusions of previous generations to change.

The Church is not the only entity to see the need for looking at sexual orientation and gender in a different light. I attended a workshop by two competent professionals, one a priest, the other a nun. They explained that the scientific community no longer looks at homosexual orientation as an abnormality, but as a part of the natural diversity that is present in all of nature.

The entire field of sexual orientation and gender has exploded into a reality that is challenging but also exciting. We are now able to see huge diversity in this area, in the same way that we see diversity in all of nature and in the cosmos. (See the diagrams on pp. 64.)

If we as human beings are so arrogant as to believe that we know everything, we will not be open to new ideas and realities. For that reason, it becomes necessary for us to consider how important Principle 5 is: *It is important for others to give to you.*

4. Cosmic Intelligence

Brian Swimme is a cosmologist who has made a lasting impression on my view of reality. He explains that we used to think of outer space as being a vacuum. In reality, quantum physics shows that outer space is a sea of infinite potential. Everywhere in the universe, even in our immediate presence, the smallest particles of reality are seething with creativity. Electrons and other particles inside each atom are constantly blinking in and out of existence, ever ready to form into whatever Creative Intelligence directs. You and I are connected to that Creative Intelligence, and when we visualize any reality, that mental act becomes a command for the infinite sea of potentiality to create. We truly are co-creators of all reality! What an awesome subject for meditation!

If you want to read some beautiful and challenging poems or meditations on these cosmic realities, spend some time with Ed Hays' *Psalms for Zero Gravity!* I also recommend watching *The Awakening Universe* (DVD) by Neal Rogin and listening to *The Power of the Universe* (CDs) by Brian Swimme.

5. Origin of the Human Species

Another unique and exciting discovery of the last two centuries is the origin of the human species. Dr. Spencer Wells is a geneticist who spent 10 years following the journey of human DNA, which began 50,000 years ago in Africa. Using the science of genetics, he and his colleagues were able to pinpoint the exact place where our human ancestors first lived and how, when, and why they moved from Africa all the way to Australia, then into Europe and Asia, and eventually into North and finally South America. These studies are another clear proof that all humans on the planet come from one source and that we are all related.

The science of genetics came into being at the exact time when it would be possible to trace our human lineage. If this discovery had not happened until several generations later, it would have been impossible to do the studies that have been completed today. The amazing truth is that we now know that divisions in human society like "Russians," "Americans," "Indians," "Australians," etc., are only a figment of human imagination. The fact is, we are one family, coming from the same parents, and proof of that reality is in the DNA of our cells!

If you want to get further documentation on this amazing reality, see the DVD *The Journey of Man,* featuring Dr. Wells and produced by PBS.

We of the 21st century are blessed above every generation before us to have the knowledge and understanding of the cosmos and of human development that we have! By opening ourselves to receiving the truth about ourselves, our universe, our past, and our minds, we have the opportunity to be amazed, awestruck, and transformed into beings that can be a step above *Homo sapiens*!

E. Receiving Touch

Did you know that the experts tell us that in order to be emotionally and psychologically stable, the average person needs a minimum of 12 hugs a day? What they are talking about is the need all human beings have for being touched. Touch is a basic and essential element to the health of all human beings.

We were very blessed as children in our family. My mom and dad insisted that we hug and kiss them often. We had an unwritten rule in the house. When we entered the house, we had to seek out both Ma and Daddy and give them a hug and a kiss and tell them that we were home. We did the very same thing when we left the house and always told our parents where we were going. Even today when I am with my brothers and their wives, my nieces and nephews, my cousins, the Friars, and even the staff at the Hermitage, we always hug and kiss when coming or going from the building.

I realize that there are persons who may have difficulty with this kind of lifestyle, but I do believe that it is a healthy one.

Even if a person, for any reason, has become afraid of human touch, that condition can be changed! In my book *Success: Full Thinking,* I offer a good number of techniques that anyone can use to change any aspect of his/her life. Here again is a challenge for accepting the gift of new understanding, and for using the powers of Mind for further human development.

If a person says, "I can't change," then that is the reality the person will create in his/her life. But please note, it is the thought process that creates the reality. The mind is virtually unlimited, but we have free will. We can dip into that unlimited reservoir, that infinite sea of potentiality to bring into existence anything we want! That statement is not a personal opinion; it is the teaching of scientists, theologians, and mystics alike.

After the Second World War, there was a hospital that had a huge number of babies, so many in fact that the nurses had an impossible task of taking sufficient care of them all. What they discovered over a period of time was that babies who were not frequently held and/or physically touched became ill. Many of them died. Today, it is a well documented fact that children who are held and touched will be more psychologically and emotionally healthy. For years, the medical profession has admitted to and taught the art and power of healing touch.

Just the other day I heard about a set of twins. One was born very strong and healthy, but the other was weak and frail. Both were in incubators, but the weak one was not improving; in fact the baby was getting weaker every day. A nurse who had heard of the bonding that happens with twins thought that perhaps if both babies were in the same incubator, the weak one would fare better. After asking the parents for permission, the nurse put the two infants together. The healthy one was found to have its arm around the weak one, and as time went on, the weak infant got better and eventually became strong and healthy. What medicine could not do, physical touch was able to do.

Consider how natural it is for a husband to comfort a wife by holding her in his arms. This is true also of a friend who wants to comfort another friend at the death of a loved one, or on the occasion of a serious accident or other disturbing news. People instinctively embrace each other and actually do transfer healing energy to each other.

Here in the United States, touching is not always that easy. Many, today, are being taught not to touch. In some cases, the law forbids touching. However, in other countries, embracing and kissing are part of the culture, and even public officials greet one another with these gestures.

When I first entered the Order, touching was forbidden. In my judgment, there was so much fear about sex that any kind of touching was suspect (not a healthy attitude!). However, when family came to visit me, we always hugged and kissed. The first time that this happened, I was called to the Rector's office and told that I could not be involved in those kinds of activities anymore because it was a sin. I was shocked to say the least, but in the back of my mind, I was saying, "There is something wrong here!"

I never stopped hugging and kissing, and as the years went on, more and more of the Friars were comfortable with physically touching so that now it is very common for all of the Friars to hug and sometimes kiss to express our brotherly affection. In my estimation, this kind of custom and practice is healthy and, I feel, an important and necessary part of all human communication and contact.

Even in our liturgies, I suggest when we pray the Our Father that we join hands as a sign of our unity. There are still some members of congregations who are not comfortable with this kind of touching, but I have no doubt that as we move into the future, touching will be more acceptable and more comfortable for everyone. "*Noli me tangere!*" is the Latin phrase for "Don't touch me!" That expression became a law and kept priests and religious apart physically for centuries. Thank God it is an expression that died and is buried!

If you have a problem with accepting physical touch, you might think of going to a therapeutic massage person. Stephanie Simonton, author of *Getting Well Again,* has worked with cancer patients for decades. She highly recommends massage as part of cancer therapy. Professionals in the field know how to project healing energy through their hands during a massage and can promote emotional and spiritual healing while working on the body.

At one point, here at the Hermitage, we had a nun, Sr. Fran, who was a professional massage person. Some of her clients came every week because the spiritual boost they got helped them significantly in dealing with stress in their daily lives.

Some years ago, I received a whole series of massage treatments known as Rolfing. It is a deep kind of massage directed especially to put the fascia back into its proper position. It was an amazing experience. When the therapist was working on my right eye, the memory of an injury to that eye came back to me in vivid images. I was only 4 or 5 years old, playing football with my cousins and my brothers. During the game I ran into my cousin's belt buckle; that created a rather large cut just above my eye. That memory was buried in the cells of that eye and when stimulated by massage, it brought back the experience in great detail. This kind of flashback happened when other parts of my body were treated, and I experienced several kinds of emotional and spiritual, as well as physical, healing.

F. Find God in Pleasure

The sense of touch is essential to every human being. The skin is the largest organ of the body and is given to us for pleasure. In his book *Whee, We, Wee, All the Way Home,* Matthew Fox explains how bodily pleasure is an important God contact. Fox explains how Creation Spirituality is built on the premise that we experience God in a special way in pleasure – and our skin is an important part of that experience. Even the Vatican Council in the Catholic Church spoke of the importance of pleasure as one of the ends of marriage. The Council was clear that having children, mutual support, shared love and companionship, as well as pleasure all have an equal value in marriage. I know that is true in any relationship! We were made for pleasure, and our very humanness drives us toward pleasure because it is there that we can experience the Divine in a special way.

While doing a Vipassana Meditation retreat, we were taught how to get the most pleasure out of eating. We were to take only small amounts of food into our mouths, chewing very slowly while consciously paying attention to the experience of the food in our mouths, distinguishing the different tastes of the food, and getting the most that we could out of the experience. To this very day, I take pleasure in the food that I eat; I have learned to eat slowly and to savor every bite. Ironically, this approach to eating is not only enjoyable, it is very healthy!

I would like to recall for you, at this point, an old Jewish teaching: You will all be accountable to God for the pleasurable opportunities that were given to you, but which you did not use!

If you already know how to receive pleasure through the sense of touch, you can always develop more skill. If you have a difficulty accepting pleasure through the sense of touch, start with the meditation process and mentally see yourself being comfortable as you experience the pleasure of physical touch. Once you begin the process in your mind, it will be only a matter of time before you will have the experience in the physical world!

G. Application

1. Create a habit of saying, "Thank you!"
   when you receive an honest compliment (no excuses or explanations!)
2. Accept gifts graciously.
3. Listen carefully to someone who has different values or ideas.
4. Expose yourself to different views and beliefs.
5. When someone offers a helping hand, accept graciously.

PRINCIPLE
6

Difficulty and Pain Are Opportunities
for Growth

Everyone experiences difficulty and pain daily. The question here is this: What to do with difficulty and pain? Children do not want to deal with any life experience that is unpleasant. As soon as they experience any discomfort, they cry to let parents know they are not comfortable, or they try to run away from the experience, or they try to fight it by getting angry, etc. The only reason that children run away from any kind of discomfort is that they do not understand the purpose and value of difficulty and pain in our life experience. They interpret any uncomfortable experience as "bad" and do whatever they can to get rid of it.

Unfortunately, much of our culture is based on the same thought process. We are led to believe that unpleasant experiences are "bad" and that pleasant experiences are "good." The reality is that unpleasant, uncomfortable, difficult, and even painful experiences are always opportunities for growth of one kind or another.

I was only about 3 years old when Leota came to our house to babysit my brother and me. My folks were going out for the evening, and when I realized that they were leaving, I began to cry uncontrollably. It was so painful that I remember it vividly to this day.

Looking at the situation from a more mature point of view, it is a good and healthy thing for a child to feel comfortable away from parents. In fact, it is necessary for any child to learn to be comfortable separated from his/her parents. This kind of uncomfortable experience I described above leads a child toward maturity and independence.

Even physical pain is a sign that something in the body is not functioning properly and alerts the person to do whatever it takes to "fix" the situation. For example, when a person becomes very tense, the blood vessels in the body and the brain constrict and can create a headache. The pain in the head is a wonderful sign the body creates to let the person know he/she is not controlling stress.

Physical pain can also lead to healing. My mom, as a young adult, fell and broke a bone in her left elbow. The bone healed quite nicely, and she went back to a normal life. Then, one day, she fell again and broke the same bone! This time the doctors had to put a metal rod in the joint to make the arm operable again. The doctor told my grandfather that the arm would have to be exercised every day for months if Ma was to get flexibility back into that elbow again. Ma told me how painful it was when her dad forced that arm to bend a little bit more each day; how she cried and begged Grandpa not to make her suffer so much. However, when the therapy was complete, my Mom had near normal use of that arm. She never recovered complete motion, but few ever noticed that she had some limited movement in her elbow. If she had not endured the pain, she would not have had the quality of life that was hers till she died.

A. Ken and Cindy

Ken, a good friend of many years, was going through extremely difficult times in his marriage, family, and personal life. For years he had to deal with family illness, financial challenges, emotional and psychological stress, as well as personal struggles. Through it all, I saw him work with Principle 6 with such success that I asked if he would be willing to share his story. Here is what he wrote:

> For over 20 years I had to deal with a seriously dysfunctional marriage and the trauma and turmoil connected with it. After our divorce, I spent

considerable time in meditation. I wanted to assess what happened, why it happened, and how I could use all of that experience to build my future. I recalled painful experiences of growing up in a single-parent home with my mother, who was addicted to both drugs and alcohol. I also remembered that in my late teens, I realized the fact that I could make choices but that I would have to pick up the responsibility of those choices. I embraced the adage that "it's not important what happens in life, but what you do with what happens that is paramount." With that attitude, I gained my undergraduate degree from Wabash College in only three years and then went on to achieve my master's degree.

Reflecting on these successes, I realized that I had the capacity to be successful again. I was now focused on creating a new chapter in my life. I made a point of keeping my attitude positive and concentrated on helping all the people who were in my life and the new ones that entered my life every day. Always thinking in terms of a new and better relationship for me and my children, I looked for things that could assist me in my search.

One day I came across a poem that made a powerful impact on me.

The Invitation

It doesn't interest me what you do for a living. I want to know what you ache for, and if you dare to dream of meeting your heart's longing.

It doesn't interest me how old you are. I want to know if you will risk looking like a fool for love, for your dream, for the adventure of being alive.

It doesn't interest me what planets are squaring your moon. I want to know if you have touched the center of your own sorrow, if you have been opened by life's betrayals or have become shriveled and closed from fear of further pain. I want to know if you can sit with pain, mine and your own, without moving to hide it or fade it or fix it.

I want to know if you can be with joy, mine or your own, if you can dance with wildness and let the ecstasy fill you to the tips of your fingers and toes without cautioning us to be careful, to be realistic, to remember the limitations of being human.

It doesn't interest me if the story you are telling me is true. I want to know if you can disappoint another to be true to yourself; if you can bear the accusation of betrayal and not betray your own soul; if you can be faithless and therefore trustworthy.

I want to know if you can see beauty, even when it's not pretty, every day, and if you can source your own life from its presence.

I want to know if you can live with failure, yours and mine, and still stand on the edge of the lake and shout to the silver of the full moon, "Yes!"

It doesn't interest me to know where you live or how much money you have. I want to know if you can get up, after the night of grief and despair, weary and bruised to the bone, and do what needs to be done to feed the children.

It doesn't interest me who you know or how you came to be here. I want to know if you will stand in the center of the fire with me and not shrink back.

It doesn't interest me where or what or with whom you have studied. I want to know what sustains you, from the inside, when all else falls away.

I want to know if you can be alone with yourself and if you truly like the company you keep in empty moments.

—Oriah Mountain Dreamer

One day, while having my hair cut, I read it to my hairdresser. I told her that if she ever ran across a woman who would understand this poem in her "bone marrow," I would love to meet her.

Not long after, she called me, telling me that she would like to introduce me to a friend named Cindy. On January 20, 2006, we met for the first time and spent hours in conversation over a long and relaxed meal. Cindy had raised two boys by herself, without any financial or emotional assistance from her ex-husband. She had been out in the dating world for more than 20 years and was at a point where she really didn't care if she met another man. She felt her life was full, given her faith, her boys, her deep friendships, and her two "roommates," Bailey (a yellow lab and soulmate) and Jave (a pit bull she had rescued while living on St. Croix).

With the excitement of that first meeting, I did not want to act impulsively or too quickly, as I had done with my first marriage, so I fought off the urges and waited a week to call Cindy for a second date. Thereafter, we spent considerable time together discussing a full range of topics, doing a variety of activities: theater, canoeing, sporting events, a variety of travel experiences, etc.

During this courting period, we introduced and spent some time with each other's children. We all fit together like peas in a pod. In February of 2007, I proposed to Cindy in Puerto Vallarta (one of her favorite cities), and she said, "Yes!"

We were married October 14, 2007, in Las Vegas, where her boys live. Her oldest walked her down the aisle, and our new family was born.

To this day, we continue to respect each other's feelings; we discuss whatever is on our minds without judgment or reservation, and have become each other's best friend! We know we can count on each other and feel very fortunate and blessed!

What is even more exciting, Cindy's boys have found a father, my children have a loving, supportive mother, and all of us have bonded into a truly wonderful family!

Ken, Cindy, and Their New Family

These are a few of the many lessons we have learned:
1. What happens is not as important as what one does with what happens!
2. The start of any new event requires a shift in attitude.
3. Meditation is invaluable and allows one to get in touch with the Divine, be it for solace, inspiration, or direction.
4. *Pain is an important energy to which one must direct reflection. It is important, or it wouldn't be painful. Far more can be learned from what is bothersome or painful, than what is easy or pleasant.*
5. Relationships are how we are defined, but they are also the most meaningful dimension of our lives. Relationships take considerable time and energy. Our relationship with the Divine is where we can get direction for and clarity about our relationships.

In my estimation, the above is a clear example of how difficult and challenging life experiences were used to gain maturity, prepare two individuals for bigger and better life experiences, and create understanding of and appreciation for the process of life!

In my own life, I realize the value of the difficult and challenging experiences that I have had to encounter. I had wanted for years to take a sabbatical and really needed to show down a bit. After deciding on a time and place for a year off, I began to find ways and means to gather the funds that would make a sabbatical possible. I applied for a grant from our Provincial Office, requested financial help from the constituency of the Hermitage, and created an account that would be used only for support of my sabbatical.

After almost two years of preparation, I was ready and eager to move to Italy, where I intended to live at the Franciscan Graduate School of St. Anthony in Rome. I was eager to study Italian but at the same time to take courses in spirituality, which is my passion.

I had been in Rome for several weeks, and everything was going beautifully, until I got an e-mail from the Hermitage. The e-mail explained that the Board of Directors decided to hire a Director for a significant salary. I knew that the Center could not support that kind of financial output, so I requested a budget from the Board that would show from where the money was to come.

The person who was to take the position convinced the Board that she could generate the income necessary for her salary. She also suggested that I be removed temporarily from the Board since I was living in Rome, and it would take too much time to communicate with me. At the next meeting of the Board, I was removed from my position as Founding Director of the Hermitage, even though the bylaws had given me a life membership on the Board.

When I began to ask questions about all of the changes that were being made, I was told that I was being negative, and that I was to act with faith in the Board Members and in the new Director. Only one of the volunteers, who was handling the financial account for my sabbatical, remained loyal to me and kept me informed of what was happening.

The new Director proceeded to spend all of the money in the Hermitage checking account and then began to borrow from the Hermitage savings account in increments of $5,000. By the time I was into the ninth month of my sabbatical, I got word that the Hermitage was running out of funds.

I had to break my sabbatical and come back to the States to see what could be done about the situation. When I arrived, I discovered that several members of the Board had been fired, or left on their own, and that the Chairman of the Board was now a fundamentalist minister. This Chairman was busy trying to get new members for the Board from his own constituency, so that he could take over the Hermitage, and its tax-exempt status, for his ministry and congregation.

The next weeks were some of the most difficult of my professional career. I had put my entire life into the Hermitage for 17 years, and now was faced with the possibility of losing it. I felt like a parent fearing for the life of a child.

Only two people on the Board were willing to help regain ownership of the Hermitage, and a fellow Friar from St. Louis was willing to join in this important project.

We were able to regain control of the Hermitage, but we had no money to support the buildings and the property. Our bylaws stated that in the event of dissolution, the first entity of receivership would the Franciscan Province of the Sacred Heart, since it was the Province that allowed me to start the Hermitage, and the entity that gave us the moral and spiritual support we needed to continue our work.

The Board then gave all of the property and buildings to the Province, but we were able to preserve the Hermitage as a tax-exempt, not-for-profit entity.

Since the Province was allowing two religious persons to occupy the main building for use as a house of prayer, I felt blessed when we were allowed to use half of the laundry room in the basement for the Hermitage office. With this arrangement, we were able to keep our phone number, our fax number, and our address. The Hermitage was reduced to essentials and nothing more, but we were able to continue our work, even on an international level. Another blessing was that the Province allowed me to continue to live in the Friary, which had been built by the Hermitage and was located only 500 feet east of the main building.

Throughout this ordeal, I was tempted to blame everyone else. But applying *Principle 6, Difficulty and pain are opportunities for growth,* I knew that I had to look ahead and build a new future. Fortunately, I continued to teach *Success: Full Living* and *Success: Full Thinking.* These programs forced me to think and talk about goal-setting, positive attitude, and the use of meditation.

As I refocused toward the future, I became excited about creatively building a new reality, and the Hermitage began a new and wonderful chapter in its life! Every day I was making significant changes. I moved my office to the Friary. More volunteers became involved in our ministry. Speaking invitations came from all over the States, Europe, and Australia. I had to shoulder more responsibility, but that was helping me understand our ministry better.

I frequently reflected on the principle of this chapter: *Difficulty and pain are opportunities for growth* – and grow I did! I began to use the meditation on *Healing Relationships* on a regular basis to mend my connection with everyone involved. I made sure that I continued to exercise daily, and to attend support groups to which I belong.

I became more aware of the fact that I did not have to generate as much income for salaries or for maintenance of, and insurance for, the buildings and property. My concentration focused on the wonderful people around me, who gave me the moral and spiritual support I needed to move on. Over the next seven years, I was able to see personal and spiritual growth that I had never before achieved.

At present, we are back in the Hermitage House, and we have two part-time employees. I appreciate, more than ever, the stability of having a place and the excitement of people coming regularly to join us in the process of personal growth and development.

As I look back on those challenging years, I am grateful to all the people who made those growth opportunities possible. It is easier for me to see the perfect plan of God for me and for the Hermitage.

Perhaps you, the reader, can take the sharing of this personal experience as a stimulant to look into your own life, where you might be experiencing pain and/or suffering. Look objectively at these situations as opportunities, and find a way to use them for your personal growth and development. These are the life experiences that always lead to inner strength, clear values, and insight into what is really important!

Thank God for the challenging times in our lives. They can be the greatest blessings we could ever receive!

Prayer, of course, is a great tool for turning difficult and painful experiences into opportunities for growth. Ho'oponopono is a prayer form that I use almost daily. Perhaps this can be a useful tool for you too.

B. Ho'oponopono

Let me begin with a story about a therapist who was working in Hawaii. His name is Dr. Ihaleakala Hew Len. He was assigned to a hospital ward for the criminally insane and has a very unique way of helping patients without ever being with them physically. He believes in the universal connection of all things and the mutual connection and effect of all things on one another. When he picked up a chart of one of the patients, he reflected on the fact that the fault in the patient was, to some degree, in his own person. His belief was that if he could, in meditation, ask for forgiveness from the patient and deal with healing in himself, the patient, also, could be affected with healing.

For example, if he were thinking of a very violent patient, he thought of times in his own life when he was violent. In his office he would go into meditation, visualize the patient in front of him, and repeat this mantra over and over again: "I am sorry; please forgive me." He believed that by admitting to and healing his own violence, he could help the patient to heal his/her violence.

This approach may seem strange to any reader who does not understand the oneness of the universe.

Most people, I believe, think that they can be responsible for themselves, but they cannot be responsible for others. However, in the world of quantum physics and the holographic model of the universe, that statement is not true.

Dr. Len worked at a state hospital in Hawaii for four years. There, the ward for the criminally insane was a very dangerous place. Some professionals on that floor left within a month of beginning their jobs. Support staff often called in sick, or quit, because they were in fear the whole time they were at work. Some would not walk through the ward without keeping their backs to the wall, in order to keep an eye on everyone; so strong was their fear of being attacked. That ward was, indeed, a dangerous place.

Dr. Len never physically went to the ward. Instead, he sat in his office and examined the patients' files one at a time. With a file in front of him, he would go into meditation, imagine the fault of the patient as an exaggeration of the same fault he could see in himself. Then he would mentally repeat the mantra: "I am sorry; please forgive me."

Using this prayer technique daily, Dr. Len began to see changes in the patients, even though he had not had any physical contact with them. Patients who were shackled were being allowed to be with other patients. Those who were on heavy medication were using less, and in some cases getting away from drugs altogether. Other patients, who seemingly had no chance for recovery, were regaining their health.

Of course, in this changed environment, the staff was feeling more at ease, turnover virtually disappeared, and the ward began to have a surplus of staff because patients were being released. In the end, the ward was closed because everyone was cured!

When asked, "What were you doing within yourself that changed those people?" Dr. Len responded, "I was simply healing the part of me that created them." You can understand this answer if you realize that all of the cosmos is connected; it is a single reality, created by a single intelligence, to which we are all connected. In a very real sense, we do create the world in which we live!

I realize that this kind of thinking may be new to some, but in the Matriarchal Model of spirituality, we are all connected, we are all one. The scientific community has documented and proved this reality. The logical conclusion following from this truth is this: We have responsibility for life, all of it! There is only one Life Principle; therefore, what each of us sees, hears, feels, tastes, or touches is our creation. That means when we hear of terrorist bombings, or weakness in the economy, or shootings on the street, or any other experience we don't like, it's up to us to heal it! We perceive these realities, and that means they exist in us. So, if we heal these perceptions in ourselves, the reality changes, and external healing happens.

As you read these words, you might have the same response as the listeners of Jesus, who said, "Master, this is a hard saying; who can listen to it?" What we are saying here is that when we heal ourselves, we heal the reality that we have created. It is so easy to blame others for the reality that we see and experience. It takes a lot of effort to shift thought process and accept the responsibility of making changes that can make our world a better place. By going into meditation, reflecting on the change we want to see, and then actually making that change in our own minds and hearts, we *can* change ourselves and our world.

Joe Vitale, author of *The Attractor Factor* and *The Zero Factor,* relates how one day he received an e-mail that he allowed to upset him. Before his contact with Ho'oponopono, he would have approached the challenge by quieting himself and trying to reason with the person by another e-mail. However, this time he decided to use the prayer of Ho'oponopono, going into meditation, and mentally repeating over and over again, "I'm sorry; please forgive me." Within an hour's time, he received another e-mail from the person apologizing for his previous communiqué. Joe hadn't contacted the person; he simply used the prayer of Ho'oponopono.

Quantum physics, as well as other departments of science and philosophy, question whether there is an "out there" away from us. All we, as human beings, can know is what our personal experience is, and all of that is "inside." In this mental framework, it is logical to conclude that by healing anything within ourselves, we are actually healing or changing all that we sense as "out there."

The practical application is simple. All reality is within each of us, and we have the power, through our use of Mind, to change any of it. All we have to do is go within, check out the reality we experience, and generate love! In the words of Dr. Ihaleakala Hew Len:

> Ho'oponopono is really very simple. For the ancient Hawaiians, all problems begin as thought. But having a thought is not the problem. So what's the problem? The problem is that all our thoughts are imbued with painful memories of persons, places, or things. The intellect working alone can't solve these problems, because the intellect only manages. Managing things is no way to solve problems. What you want to do is let them go! When you do Ho'oponopono, what happens is that the Divinity takes the painful thought and neutralizes, or purifies, it. You don't purify the person, place, or thing. You neutralize the energy you associate with that person, place, or thing. So, the first stage of Ho'oponopono is the purification of that energy.
>
> After that, something wonderful happens; not only does that energy get neutralized, it also gets released, so there is now a brand-new state. Buddhists call this state the Void.
>
> The final step is that you allow the Divinity to come in and fill the Void with light. To do Ho'oponopono you don't have to know what the problem or error is. All you have to do is notice any problem you are experiencing physically, mentally, emotionally, or whatever. Once you notice, your responsibility is to immediately begin to clean by saying, "I am sorry. Please forgive me!"

When you know about a technique like Ho'oponopono, and especially after you have used it, you will know from your own experience that every challenge in life is an opportunity to grow into a better person, into an instrument of peace, and into a model for others to follow!

Perhaps the comparison with the human body can help. The body is made up of billions of cells, all of which have intelligence. Each of these cells is communicating constantly with all the other cells in the body. Some of these cells know how to be skin cells; others know how to be heart cells, etc. But once the cells bond together to form an organ, there is still another level of intelligence functioning in that organ. For example, blood knows how to deposit toxins into the liver and the kidneys, and the liver and the kidneys know how to get toxins out of the body.

When the body is injured, there still another level of intelligence that causes all the parts of the body to work together to deliver healing to the damaged part, and bring the entire body back to perfect health. But even beyond the body, there is the intelligence of the person who is expressing through the body – an intelligence that can communicate with the intelligence of other persons. We can go beyond each person, and experience another level of intelligence in which all human beings value love, joy, peace, etc. Finally, we get to Cosmic Intelligence, which has created the universe, continues to create, and even expand, the universe. We speak of different levels of Intelligence, but there is only one Intelligence.

When you can image Intelligence in this way, it will be easier for you to realize why Ho'oponopono works. All reality is one. In this model, there is a principle that states the center of the universe is everywhere, the circumference is nowhere. That means, when you go into meditation, you are the center of the universe, and you can communicate with the cosmos and every part of it. Your thoughts, then, affect everyone and everything in the cosmos. Positive thoughts move the entire universe in a positive direction. Negative thoughts move the universe in a negative direction.

All of the above will only give you intellectual understanding of Ho'oponopono. The next step is to *do* Ho'oponopono so that you get the personal experience. (See available recordings in the "Reference Materials" at the end of this volume.)

C. Choir of Hard Knocks

Here is an example of a talented gentleman who took a difficult situation and turned it into something beautiful. For 30 years, Jonathon Welch has been acclaimed as one of the finest tenors of his time. Having performed internationally, he more recently extended his career to teaching and choral conducting. He returned to his hometown of Melbourne, Australia, where he became intrigued by an article in *Reader's Digest* about a choir in Montreal, Canada, that had been created for homeless people. He connected with RecLink, a charitable organization that organizes sport and recreational activities for the homeless and disadvantaged. They agreed to support Jonathon's project for a "Choir of Hard Knocks" created especially for the homeless. He began by putting out fliers in the streets of Melbourne, visiting crisis centers and hostel accommodations as well as working with local agencies.

The first night scheduled for a rehearsal, Jonathon waited, not knowing if anyone would appear. To his joy, 20 people came, and within a few weeks the number had grown to 50. They produced a wonderful CD that created the income they needed to put on a concert at the Melbourne Town Hall for an audience of 1,600.

The choir meets every Wednesday afternoon for rehearsals, and RecLink helps to channel income not only for the benefit of the choir, but more important, to get lives back on track. Choir members are assisted to enter rehabilitation programs, to find jobs, to settle into adequate housing, etc.

Their first CD, *Choir of Hard Knocks*, and their second album, *Songs of Hope and Inspiration*, are available nationwide as well as on the Internet. Jonathon recently completed an album of his own titled *With a Song in My Heart.*" With all of this success, the Choir of Hard Knocks continues to perform, continues to build lives, and continues to bring beauty, hope, and enjoyment to millions of people around the globe.

My hope is that these stories will help the reader realize that all human beings are connected to Creative Intelligence, and it is this Intelligence that can help us to turn *any* challenging situation into an opportunity for personal growth and development. I pray that parents, pastors, educators, day-care professionals, psychologists, etc., will understand *Principle 6, Difficulty and pain are opportunities for growth,* put it into practice in their personal lives, and teach it to all our children!

D. Application

1. Name a person who is a challenge in your life at the present time.

_____

_____

_____

How can you deal with this person so that both of you grow and mature?

_____

_____

_____

2. Describe a challenging situation with which you are dealing at the present time.

_____

_____

_____

How can you use this situation for greater personal growth and development?

_____

_____

_____

3. Get a copy of *Choir of Hard Knocks* and/or *Songs of Hope and Inspiration* (www.choirofhardknocks.com.au) and share this success story with others.

4. Try using the prayer of Ho'oponopono to make your life better, as well as the lives of others.

PRINCIPLE 7

The Divine Plan Is Perfect

This final principle is perhaps one of the most challenging of all. It suggests that you accept everything in life that comes your way without judgment, knowing that all life experience is valuable and every life situation can lead to a full life.

In the mystical tradition, this kind of awareness is referred to as the Contemplative Model. It is a state in which human beings consciously live in the present moment. It is a state that can be achieved by mind discipline and can be developed by anyone. It is a state in which human beings can be at perfect peace and in love with all reality. It is the mindset of Jesus, Buddha, Gandhi, Mother Teresa, as well as holy people of all major religions. In this awareness, we can "see" God's plan as perfect. In this awareness, there are no mistakes. In this awareness, there is only one reality, Love!

Eckhart Tolle, in his book *The Power of Now,* explains this state of awareness, how it can be achieved and what its value is. Tolle is not offering anything new; he is simply giving a modern presentation of the Contemplative Model that has been part of the mystical tradition of all religions for millennia.

Both Richard Rohr, OFM, and Thomas Keeting, OCSO, have a wonderful presentation of this material in their series titled *The Eternal Now (And How to Be There)*. Whether we are conscious of it or not, all human beings are heading in the direction of the Contemplative Model. It is the state in which we will find our ultimate purpose, and where we connect with the Divine in a transformative way. Once we experience this state, the application of Principle 7 is simple: *expect the best – demand nothing.* Perhaps the following story will help you understand the mindset that is attached to Principle 7 and what the practical application is.

A. Ahhhhhhhhhhhh Soooooooooooo

This story comes from a volume that was handed to me by one of my fellow Friars when I was a young priest and educator. The story takes place in the Far East. An elderly gentleman has lost his wife to death, and his children are grown, with their own families. He feels called to be a "holy man." In his culture there is a process for making this kind of change in life. He puts all of his physical assets into cash, places it on a cart, and bridles a donkey to the cart. He then allows the donkey to go in whatever direction it chooses. Every time he meets someone, he gives away some of his money. When all of the money is gone, he gives away the cart, and finally he gives away the donkey. Wherever he is at that point in time, he believes is the place where he is to live as a "holy man" for the rest of his life.

After giving away the donkey, he finds himself outside a small town at the edge of a wooded area. There he begins to gather the materials he needs to build a little hut. The people going in and out of the town report his presence to the townsfolk, who become very excited because they do not have a holy man in their area.

They immediately go out to help the old man build his hut and let him know that they will provide for all of his needs. All he has to do is to be their holy man, available to them for spiritual support, and the person who can share his wisdom with everyone in the town.

The holy man, being very detached from material things and human values, puts his hands up on both sides of his head and says, "Ahhhhhhhhhhhh soooooooooooo!" (which is his way of saying; "That's the way it is!").

Illustrations by Bertin Miller, OFM

Ahhhhhhhhhhhh

Illustrations by Bertin Miller, OFM

Soooooooooooo

After some time, a young, unmarried girl in the village is found to be pregnant, and everyone is horrified. When asked who the father of the child is, she points to the holy man.

The villagers are angered and feel betrayed. They rush out to the holy man and denounce him as a fraud. Then they inform him that when the child is born, he will have to leave, take the baby with him into the mountains, and never return.

The holy man, always accepting what comes, simply puts up his hands and says,: "Ahhhhhhhhhhh soooooooooooo!" (That's the way it is!).

When the child is born, the townspeople take the baby to the holy man and watch him disappear into the mountains.

Some years later, the mother of this child is dying and tells the people that the holy man was not the father of her child. She accused him because she wanted to protect her young lover.

The people realize that they have made a serious mistake and perpetrated a grave injustice on the holy man. They gather a few men as envoys, who are to go into the mountains looking for the holy and to make restitution.

When they find the holy man, the child has become a young adult. The messengers tell the holy man that they have made a grave mistake and committed a serious injustice toward him. They tell him that they realize, now, that he is truly a holy man and that they want him to return. They promise to take care of him for the rest of his life. His only response is "Ahhhhhhhhhhh soooooooooooo!" ("That's the way it is!").

The teaching contained in the story is simple: Accept everything in life without getting upset.

Let's move the story into the 21st century. Suppose you come home after work and open your mail to find that you have won a million-dollar sweepstakes drawing. If you are a truly contemplative person and, like the holy man, can accept whatever comes, you too can put up your hands and simply say: "Ahhhhhhhhhhh soooooooooooo! What will I do with this million dollars?"

On the other hand, suppose you come home one day to find that while at work your house has burned down, and you have lost everything. If you are truly a contemplative person and, like the holy man, can accept whatever comes, you can put up your hands and simply say, "Ahhhhhhhhhhh soooooooooooo! Where will I sleep tonight?"

A more practical application could be like this. A husband and wife have been invited to a party after work. The husband knows exactly what he will wear, but when he goes to his drawer, he finds that the socks that he needs for his suit are not there. Turning to his wife, he shouts, "Where did you hide my socks?"

The wife, being of a more contemplative mindset, puts up her hands, saying, "Ahhhhhhhhhhhh soooooooooooo, I sense that you are angry." Of course, when you have one person who has the mindset of the holy man, it is impossible to have an argument.

I must say that this little technique has worked for us here at the Hermitage. I was preparing to leave for an extended speaking tour in Australia and was racing all over the building collecting the pieces I needed for my programs. Several times I went down the staircase past the receptionist's desk, where our faithful volunteer Bert Conreau sat answering the phones. After several of these hurried passes in the corridor, Bert stood at the bottom of the staircase facing me with her hands in the air, and she simply said, "Ahhhhhhhhhhhh soooooooooooo." She didn't have to say anything else. We both started laughing, and I was able to calm myself and go about my packing in a more humane manner

I believe that the entire universe is part of a perfect plan that continues to unfold for the good of everyone and everything. Consider 13.7 billion years, and we are the universe reflecting on itself. What a mind-boggling reality. How can we not "expect the best and demand nothing"?

Here is a story from another student of mine. I think it is a good example of the perfect plan that is at work in all our lives and how Principle 7 works.

B. Ron and Lorri: A Love Story

Relationships with other people form the spiritual web of our lives.

—Frederic and Mary Ann Brussat

As dutiful parents, Ron and Lorri Kovach taught their respective children the life lesson that their own parents taught them: that with everyone you encounter in your life, that in all relationships, you must always treat others as compassionately as possible and with the utmost respect and dignity. After all, one never knows at the time how a relationship may come to bear on one's future or how a past relationship can come into play and change your life forever. This story is certainly one where such lessons ring true.

This story begins in the summer of 1973 in a sleepy, southwestern Ohio college town. Even now, Lorri says she and Ron were always connected. From the first moment he saw her, he understood the meaning of the word "smitten." Up until that point, it was only a word he read in novels, as he was an English major in college. He even used that term in a story he submitted for his Creative Writing project that summer. He often used that term trying to describe the woman he met on the first day of classes; the one with whom he quickly fell in love.

She was waiting in the residence hall line to check in for the semester; he was on the hall staff and working the desk, handing out keys. She caught his eye while the line was several people deep. The year was 1973, and she wore a white peasant blouse with red embroidery, jean cutoffs, and a red bandana. He kept stealing glances of her as she inched her way through the line up to the desk. He mustered up the courage to engage in some small talk as she leaned on the desk, and he asked her out for a beer at the end of the day. She accepted.

The summer of 1973 forever changed the lives of Ron Kovach and Lorri Strachman. They spent most of their time outside of class with each other. The rolling hills of Athens, Ohio, were perfect for summer bike rides, hikes, picnics, and the like. The usually bustling college town went into a summer slumber as the pace slowed to a crawl. Many businesses shut down or reduced their hours. Fewer students walked the brick streets, and with less distraction, two college students, he from Ohio, she from the New York City area, grew very close throughout the quiet summer weeks. The university's theater provided light, summer stock musicals among other diversions such as the local swimming lakes.

As the summer wore on, the two college students continued to fall for each other. He even brought her home one July weekend to meet his parents and family. But there was one thing he needed to tell them prior to the trip home. Even though he knew that his summer love would be welcomed warmly by his family, he was bringing her home to a devoutly Catholic family. She, however, was Jewish. His parents were not fazed, and he was relieved. They knew that he was "smitten," for his mother could always read her son, and bringing home a girl to meet his parents was not a common occurrence.

The weekend passed, but somehow made its way into his family's "folklore." Years later, his sister, for example, could always cause Ron to blush by merely speaking Lorri's name. Their time at Ron's house was also captured on his father's 8-millimeter home movie camera. They returned to campus and continued to spend most of their time together. So that they could spend even more time with each other, she got him a job where she worked that summer, in the university president's house, where they served meals at special events.

Near the end of the summer, they returned to their respective homes -- she to New York, he back to Cleveland. They wrote weekly, sent cards, and pined for each other the way that young lovers do. Both could not wait until the start of the fall term, but the end of September seemed so far off. He kept every card, every letter she sent him. She would wait every day for the postman to arrive, hoping there would be a letter with a Cleveland postmark. Both waited out the remaining months of summer until they could return to each other in the fall.

As the summer came to a close, they returned to their pastoral campus and resumed their love affair. Throughout the fall their love continued to grow deeper. She spent Thanksgiving with his family, but went out of town to student-teach in the winter before returning in the spring just before her graduation. When she finished college (he still had another year), they parted. Their separation in geographic distance and in life paths meant that eventually they would lose track of each other. After all, they were both very young, 20 years old, and not ready to make life commitment decisions. In addition, he was from a devout Catholic family, she from a strong Jewish tradition. They went their separate ways.

However, their spiritual web had been spun. Suffice it to say that their college love affair was something that affected both of their lives quite deeply. For 25 years, Ron and Lorri continued to think back with great fondness to their college love, as one tends to think about a significant person from one's past. She thought of him with great intensity over the years. Often she had the same dream over and over again. She was in a restaurant, and as the waiter brought her a glass of red wine, he also brought her a note that read, "I can see you. Ron." She would quickly stand up, wine spilling; looked for him to no avail, and woke up. This same dream came sometimes twice a year, sometimes twice a month. Although she was not certain what it meant over the years, she came to realize that he could always spiritually "see" her. Perhaps she was always looking for him, but it was cyberspace that made the search plausible.

He recalls that he would be in meetings, years later, and relish it when his mind would wander back to Lorri. He often willed these thoughts as they brought him a pleasurable diversion. While he often wondered whatever became of her, such thoughts were merely fleeting, leaving him as quickly as the warm winds of that special summer. Never in a million years could he ever imagine that their paths would ever cross again

Both eventually married others, people of their respective faiths, and both eventually divorced. Of the two, she was married first, for eight years, and gave birth to a boy and a girl. She remained single for 17 years. He was married for 17 years and was father to two sons and a daughter. He can still recall the first night he spent alone after moving out of his home. He could not have known at that time how significant that first evening alone in his new apartment would become.

That evening, having just moved into the small apartment from his beautifully-appointed suburban home in the Chicago suburbs, he knew that he left behind more than his wife of 17 years, his three young children, a dog, a pool, and all of his furniture and most of his life's possessions. Only the bare essentials could fit into a 700-square foot apartment. Although a highly-involved father of three, he knew instinctively that he would have to rework all of his relationships, and make the hard adjustment to being a divorced father with children. As dusk approached, he sat alone for what seemed like the first time in years. The shadows of darkness crept into his room while he sat in utter silence, drew a deep breath, and asked himself the simple question, "What do I do with my life now?"

Knowing that he was strong of heart and always a positive person, his first response to himself was, "When were you the happiest in your life?" He immediately thought of his college years for one simple reason. He reminded himself that this was a time when he was anxious and eager to learn everything he could. He told himself that it was time for infinite possibilities; a time when he felt that he could accomplish whatever he set his mind to do. A time when he felt most passionate about life itself and most alive. But his yearning was not nostalgia; rather, it was the feeling that he had been intellectually and spiritually alive then, that this had somehow escaped him, and this was the place to which he wished to return. In the dark silence of that night, he knew that he had to return to that place within his soul; not to that time, but rather, a new parallel. Although still in the throes of pain which his divorce dealt him, that evening had rejuvenated him. The next morning, and the next few months, would literally be the beginning of a redirected life – more than he could have ever imagined!

Her children were a few years older than his. She remained a single mother throughout their childhood. As her oldest was entering college and her youngest nearly ready to follow, she began to ask, "What is next in my life?" Her children were quick to volunteer the advice that she needed to enter the Information Age; late as it was for her, at least she was willing to begin anew. Once connected online, she was encouraged by them to learn by exploring. Among the first sites she discovered was "People Search." The first and only person that came to her mind was "Ron Kovach: where is he, and what is he doing?" She entered his name, and 36 possibilities, all with the same name, appeared, from various states. She mused, "I'll go back tomorrow and will have to call every one to find the 'right' Ron Kovach."

However, the next day, when she attempted to retrace her steps, her inexperience with technology kept her in the dark; she was unable to locate those 36. As luck would have it, she found "E-mail Search." That query produced a mere three instances of the name Ron Kovach. She claims the middle entry was surrounded by white light. Because it had "edu" at the end of the address, her instinct told her that she had found him: "I know that he is a college professor. This is him."

That day, she composed the following message, which began, "Is this the authentic Ron Kovach who attended Ohio

University the summer of 1973? These are a few things that jolt my memory bank. A Cleveland Indians ballgame, Thanksgiving dinner at your parents, and going to see the movie *Last Tango in Paris*. . . . If this the right Ron Kovach, fill me in on your life. By the way, this is Lorri Strachman."

That Friday morning in 1998, Ron went into work and found that e-mail message. It seemed surreal that someone with whom he was in love, some 25 years earlier, during his college days, would suddenly reappear in his life. He took all day to compose his response, a simple three-paragraph synopsis of his life over the past 25 years. He sent off his intense response and added: "Wow, the wonders of technology! Who would have thought some 25 years later I would have received a message from Lorri Strachman?"

After numerous e-mails and many late-night phone conversations, they found it easy to share with each other the heartbreaks of divorce and of Lorri, particularly, raising two children on her own. Within a few short months, they decided to meet. And they did.

As Ron began his flight from Chicago to meet Lorri in Washington, D.C., a reunion 25 years after they had kissed and parted in college, he prayed silently as he anticipated their reunion. He told God that he was placing whatever would happen into His hands, and an unusual calmness came over him. She was to meet him at his gate as she was scheduled to arrive first. He had wanted to meet her, but the timing was not to be. As he stepped into the waiting area, his flight being the last one at that gate for the night, no one was there to meet him! Soon, the lights of his arrival gate were turned off, and a million thoughts raced through his mind as he stood there alone, smiling at the irony of his situation. "Could she have backed out?" But such negatives were quickly dismissed, and the arrival screen confirmed that her plane from Miami, where she now lived, had not even left Florida. Neither one had cell phones then, so she had no way of informing him that he would get his wish; that is, for him to meet her plane. He would now be waiting at her gate to meet her plane, and his heart raced with anticipation of their reunion after 25 years.

He waited at her gate, leaning against a railing some 50 yards away from the door. As the passengers from her flight walked into the waiting area, he could feel his heart pounding with anticipation, waiting to see her face for the first time in all those years. He watched her look for him, and her head slowly turned as her eyes found him; everything moved to slow motion. They were drawn to each other as if by magnets, and as they stood in front of each other, their eyes locked, and they hugged with the greatest intensity as if fused to one another. He could not help thinking, "She is more beautiful than she was in college." Their first look into each other's eyes took away their breath. He felt himself fall in love with her all over again. She fell and fell hard, she would later say.

In the weekend they spent together, they shared everything about their lives, their children, their professions, their families, their heartaches, their past happiness, etc. Being alone together in a neutral city afforded them the opportunity to rekindle their young love, but now their feelings were far more intense, honed by the wisdom of experience that had forged what was quickly becoming their collective soul.

He asked her to close her eyes and put out her hands. She was curious when he told her that he had for her something from their past. She was stunned when she opened her eyes as her hands held, tied with a ribbon, the many love letters that she sent to him during the summer of 1973. He had saved every letter, every card, she had ever sent him. "Why did you keep these?" she asked. He replied, "These were a part of my life, and I held onto them, through every move to all the different places where I lived since the summer of '73, because I always felt that I might need to recall my past and write about my life someday. You were an important part of who I was, of who I am." In addition, he presented her with additional artifacts, including ticket stubs of the plays they attended, movies seen, ballgames attended. She was in awe that he had been so sentimental and had held onto these items all these years.

After two years of a long-distance relationship, traveling back and forth between Chicago and Miami, one balmy night in Florida he went on bended knee as she sat in her hammock and asked her to marry him. She said they were always connected, and she introduced him to the term "soulmate," of which, up until that point in his life, he had no emotional understanding.

They were married in March 2000. Since that time they have lived in the Chicagoland area, blended their families, seen all five of their children graduate college and three of them marry.

Soon after first reconnecting, he called his family and told them how she found him after so many years. He inquired of his mother if she still had his father's 8-millimeter home movies. She thought she did, but cautioned him that after so many years in the attic, time had likely been unkind to the film. His sister, who had over the years teased him about his college sweetheart, took the film and had it converted to tape. Today, they have a "silent" memento of that July weekend at his family's house and find much enjoyment in seeing the footage from 1973 and the "glow" they had for each other back so many years ago.

Lorri continually reminds Ron of their connection to the universe. "Think abundant and be abundant," she says to him often. He says they need only to ask of themselves: "Am I giving this other person my absolute best?" Such affirmations deepen their feelings for each other. They are each other's best friend, and each is the love of the other's life.

She knew, from the time they reconnected in the Washington area airport, that they were soulmates; he realized it, too. They feel blessed that their life paths have merged back together after a 25-year hiatus. Throughout their lives apart, they never forgot their connection, although neither of them ever thought that such a thing was possible. "The universe unfolds itself to us every day," she always told him. "But we have to use our eyes to see and our ears to hear the harmony of the spheres." The spiritual web of their lives, spun so many years ago, has continued to grow in an ever-deepening appreciation for life and love.

Ron and Lorri

Relationships with other people form the spiritual web of our lives.

—Frederic and Mary Ann Brussat

When Principle 7 becomes part of the subconscious mind, we can live with the awareness that all life experience is good. With this kind of understanding, we can live each day expecting the best of life but demanding nothing.

Of course, discipline of the thought process is essential, and we can't expect to reach that place of clear perception overnight. However, when we live with awareness, using our experience as a means of education in life, we can work through any challenge and enrich our own lives and the lives of others.

C. Ken and Barbara

Barbara Stahura has been a friend of mine for many years. When I saw her being interviewed on TV and realized how she and her husband worked through a very difficult life situation, I asked her if she would share it for this volume. Here is her story.

When my husband left for a motorcycle ride on December 29, 2003, we had no inkling our lives would be changed forever. Just a few miles from home, when he had the right of way, a white sedan turned left just yards in front of him, the driver never seeming to notice the bright red bike carrying Ken in his bulky blue jacket and blue helmet. Witnesses rushed to Ken's aid as he lay sprawled on the pavement, while the car disappeared into a busy parking lot, with no apparent concern that 600 pounds of man and metal had just collided with it. Some of Ken's injuries were apparent, but the worst was not. His helmet saved his life, but inside his skull, his jolted brain suffered traumatic injury.

For weeks, Ken could not remember anything from one minute to the next. He chatted amiably with visitors, but his words made little sense. He forgot my name for a time. He had to relearn how to dress himself, to walk without toppling over, to string words together on the page so he could read. From ICU to rehab to acute care for a pulmonary embolism, then back to rehab and finally home, Ken never gave up his struggle to come back.

I struggled, too, dealing – not always successfully – with my own pain and suffering as my husband's caregiver. We had been married exactly nine months when this sudden, horrific event left me feeling as if we'd been kidnapped to an alien world where hope of rescue was bleak. Every day I filled pages in my journal, sometimes howling with anger or grief on the page, and other times, rejoicing in some bit of progress, like the first morning Ken remembered a visit from our neighbors the night before.

We survived, and together we recovered. Ken still has some cognitive problems, but he was able to return to his job and also to continue building beautiful furniture in his wood shop. He suffered none of the terrible personality changes that can result from brain injury. His remaining physical problems are slight. We are incredibly blessed.

Three years after the accident, I was able to begin putting to use some of what I had learned after the accident. Using my experience as a freelance writer and long-time journaler, I created a journaling workshop for people with brain injury. Many studies have shown the therapeutic benefits of journaling, and I believed it would be helpful for those whose lives have been altered by brain injury.

Since then, I've been able to facilitate the six-week program twice a year, thanks to the generosity of a local rehabilitation hospital. Ken and some of the other participants have attended all the sessions, where they support and encourage one another in ways that only other survivors of head injury can do. I'm always humbled to witness their courage and determination, and thrilled to see their progress.

More recently, the workshop evolved into the first journaling book for people with brain injury, titled *After Brain Injury: Telling Your Story*, and I've also begun a journaling workshop for family caregivers. This work allows me to be of service in a way I hadn't imagined before.

I can't say what our life would have been had the driver of that white sedan not been so careless. The events of that day began a horrible time filled with pain I wouldn't wish on anyone. But at least some good has come of it, and that feels like a blessing, too.

Ken and Barbara

You may think that stories like this are rare, but that is not my experience. What I believe is that we don't take time to share our stories. Our center's website is a place where we encourage our constituents to share their stories, but we all have networks where we can share these proofs of extraordinary life experiences and how those experiences can be used to bring us joy, happiness, and fulfillment. We all have families, friends, and fellow members of support groups, churches, and business networks – all present opportunities for sharing.

Just yesterday I was listening to a conversation with Jenny McCarthy, who wrote the book *Louder than Words*. When she realized that her child was becoming autistic, she went into a panic. While talking to a friend, she was told to do something about the situation and not just complain. At that point, she began to look into books on autism, she connected with other parents who had autistic children, and she began a program for herself and her child.

By detoxifying her son and watching his diet, she was able to help her son "come back" from the world of autism. In her mind, autism in her child was not something "bad." In fact, it became a wonderful opportunity for her and for other parents with autistic children. She even got the attention of the medical community and has started a movement that will definitely change the course of autism in our world.

Look carefully at *Principle 7, The Divine Plan is perfect*. Mentally repeat this principle until it becomes a part of your subconscious. When you reach that dimension of awareness, you will be able to work with any life situation, develop a positive relationship with that experience, and move forward, telling yourself, "I can use this challenge to become a better person" or "I can use this opportunity to create a better world."

As you apply this principle and work with it on a daily basis, you will find yourself involved in life at a deep and creative level. This kind of life involvement can enrich your life as well as the lives of those around you. The challenge is controlling your thoughts, searching for solutions, and creatively giving direction to your life! That's the application of *Principle 7, The Divine Plan is perfect*.

When I encounter a difficult, even traumatic, life situation and take the time to look at it objectively, without emotion or demand, I am able to see the value of having difficult people, and challenge, in my life. That process is not always easy, and it can take time, but in the end, I am able to see love in all individuals and blessings in every life situation. I can then live in peace!

D. Application

1. Make a list of the people who love you and, in meditation, accept them as they are, especially with all their shortcomings, faults, and failings. (See the meditation *Healing Relationships*, Vol. 5.)
2. Every night before you go to sleep, count all the blessings of the day! (See the meditation, *Universal Evening Meditation*, Vol. 1.)
3. Consider one challenging aspect of your life (this could be a person) and seek ways to use this challenge as an opportunity for making you and your life better.
4, Thank God for the challenges that are present in your life! (Use "Ahhhhhhhhhhhh soooooooooooo" at least once a day!)
5, Help others, especially family and friends, to understand Principle 7 and help them to use challenges in their lives for personal growth and development.

FOLLOW-UP

Getting the information about the seven principles that govern all relationships is the easy part of personal growth. Putting these principles into practice in everyday life is where the challenge lies. In an effort to help you incorporate these ideas and principles into your thinking and then in into your life, we suggest, after reading this volume, that you work with the following suggestions on a regular basis. Ideally, it is best to work with a group of friends, or others who are interested in building healthy relationships. This chapter is dedicated to aids that you can use either with yourself or in a support group, which we refer to as a Love Circle.

A. Love Circle

A Love Circle is a group of individuals who have read this book, or are familiar with its content, or who want to learn how to be more successful with their relationships. Ideally, the group meets once a week for one hour to share how they are using the principles, and to get support from the group to continue working on relationships that are difficult or challenging. Sharing can be of many different kinds, as long as it is positive. Here is an outline of a Love Circle:

1. Review of the past week:
    Usually we begin with a few minutes of quiet, most often with meditative background music. With closed eyes, we review the past week to look for successes we have had with relationships toward self, others, things, life experiences, God, etc.

2. Personal sharing.
    Sharing can be of many different kinds, as long as it is positive.
    a. Share some positive information you encountered this week: (TV shows, movie, books, magazines, conversations, etc.).
    b. Share a success story regarding one of your own personal relationships.
    c. Describe the most positive person you met this week.
    d. Share something from yesterday that was successful.
    e. Who are the people in your life that you are given to love?
        - Who is the most difficult to love?
        - Who makes you happy?
        - What is the biggest challenge for you in any of these relationships?
        What principle(s) do you need to apply?
    f. What was the biggest blessing of the week?

3. After the sharing of personal experiences, we suggest a group meditation. Typically the meditation is one that sends healing to a specific relationship, focuses on healing a relationship (either a personal one or a relationship between two nations, or global healing), or it can focus on a relationship with a specific life experience, or with some thing or things, or with a person or persons, etc.

4. If there is time, each individual may share a challenging relationship on which he/she wishes to work during the coming week. Here are some suggestions:
    a. Have and use a support group.

b. Be positive (in thought and action).
c. Smile a lot.
d. Give compliments generously.
e. Thank people who give you good service at the supermarket, at restaurants, at work, at home, etc.
f. Work, study, play, or pray with someone with whom you want to build or heal a relationship.
g. Use meditation daily to send love to the whole world.
h. Share positive information, good experiences, etc., with others every day.
i. Describe a situation you are going to work on this week (a family member, someone at work, a challenging life situation). Consider which principle(s) you will need to use.
j. Look for the most positive person in your life this week.
k. Think of one person with whom you want to be more positive. Plan to do one or more of the following:
    i.   Send a card or letter. Let this person know you care.
    ii. Call this person on the phone.
    iii. Say "Thank you," "Please," "Congratulations," "Welcome," "I love you," "Peace and everything good!"
l. Hug as many people as you can.
m. Teach by example and only then with your words.
n. When you are angry or impatient, be silent and think positive thoughts.
o. When you see something in another person you would like to change, set a goal to change *yourself.*
p. Share only the good things you know about others.
    i.   Name someone with whom you want to be more positive.
    ii. Think about, and perhaps list, the good things you know about this person.
q. Be positive with yourself.

i.   Concentrate on your positive traits, skills, and achievements.
ii. Make a list of the above.
iii. Share your personal successes with others (both in private and in public).

5. The meeting closes with hugs and/or greetings of peace.

B. Principles of Success: Full Relating

1. There Is Beauty in Everyone and in Everything
Application: Receive all persons (including yourself) and all life situations as beautiful, exactly as they are.
Activity: Pass on some good news about yourself, someone you dislike, someone with whom you are angry, someone to whom you have been unkind.

2. You Can Change Yourself; You Cannot Change Others
Application: Become the change you want to see in others.
Activity: Choose someone with whom you want to build or improve a relationship. Do to them, or for them, what you would like for them to do to, or for, you.

3. You Can Take Control of Your Life
Application: Consciously create your own reality. Set specific goals. Think creatively about the future.
Activity: Write one goal that you would like to achieve during the next month, or next year.

4. Giving Freely Is Always Joyful
Application: Give for the pleasure of giving and not for what you can get in return.
Activity: Give some nonmaterial gift to someone you love.

5. It Is Important for Others to Give to You
Application: Provide opportunities for others to give to you.
Activity: The next time someone wants to give you something, accept graciously. Listen attentively to others who do not think the way you do.

6. Difficulty and Pain Are Opportunities for Growth
Application: See problems and challenges.
Activity: Write down the advantages of some difficulty or pain that you are experiencing at this time in your life.

7. The Divine Plan Is Perfect
Application: Expect the best – demand nothing.
Activity: Make a list of people who love you and in meditation, accept them where they are, especially with all their shortcomings, faults, and failings.

C. The Peace Prayer of St. Francis

Here is a well-known prayer that you can use in the privacy of your own home, on a train or bus, in church, in a waiting room, in stalled traffic, at the laundromat, etc. We offer it here for your convenience:

Lord, make me an instrument of your peace!
  Where there is hatred, let me sow love.
  Where there is injury, pardon.
  Where there is doubt, faith.
  Where there is despair, hope.
  Where there is darkness, light.
O Divine Master, grant that I may not so much seek
  to be consoled, as to console;
  to be understood, as to understand;
  to be loved, as to love.
For it is in giving that we receive;
  it is in pardoning that we are pardoned and
  it is in dying that we are born to eternal life!

Repeating this prayer daily will help you to see yourself as a peaceful person. Once that image is impressed on the brain, at the subconscious level, you will *be* a peaceful person! At that time, you will find yourself automatically using the principles described in this book.

D. Meditation

In my book *Success: Full Thinking* I describe how meditation is one of the most powerful tools you can use to put new information in the brain. The Franciscan Hermitage has produced 11 CDs of guided and contemplative meditations, especially for readers who have had no training in meditation. Their purpose is to help you improve relations with yourself, with others, with things, with God, and with the universe.

In my estimation, the practice of mental prayer, or meditation, is the most powerful way to put the principles of this book into your daily life. For your convenience, the catalogue of these publications can be found in the back of this volume.

EPILOGUE

As I said at the beginning of this book, my purpose in writing is to clarify and learn what I find to be so important for a full life. I believe I have a long way to go in my understanding of life and relationships, but the production of this volume has brought me to new insight and a challenging vision for the future.

Life, for me, is a great gift – but it is also an infinite mystery! We can all experience Life, but we will never be able to define it, not will we be able to fully comprehend it – in the same way that we can experience the Divine, but we will never be able to fully understand It.

I believe our task as human beings is, somehow, to mix Life and the Divine with the Cosmic Energy of Love. Only then will we find our destiny, feel what success is really like, and come to the full awareness of all that is true, good, and beautiful.

I am the first to admit that my journey toward fullness has been slow, sometimes cumbersome and halting, but always exciting. Daily I feel drawn, as if by a magnet, to Something always bigger, and better. My soul keeps stretching me into an Unknown, where Oneness is the only Reality, Love the only Power, and Peace the experience of arrival.

As I come to the end of composing these pages, I have gained more insight into the person I am and further insight into what my purpose in this life is. My hope is that having read these pages, you too have acquired greater insight into who you are and what your purpose is.

In the end, I have only the following challenge ahead of me, and that simply is this: Justin,

Know what you believe,

Live what you believe,

and

Love with abandon!

APPENDIX 1

Irena Sendler

Irena Sendler

Irena Sendler died on April 12, 2008, at the age of 98. During World War II, Irena got permission to work in the Warsaw Ghetto as a plumbing/sewer specialist. She had an "ulterior motive." She *knew* (being German) what the Nazis' plans were for the Jews. Irena smuggled infants out in the bottom of the toolbox she carried, and she carried in the back of her truck a burlap sack (for larger kids). She also had a dog in the back that she trained to bark when the Nazi soldiers let her in and out of the ghetto. The soldiers of course wanted nothing to do with the dog, and the barking covered the kids'/infants' noises. During her time of doing this, she managed to smuggle out and save 2,500 kids/infants. She was caught, and the Nazis broke both her legs and arms and beat her severely. Irena made a record of the names of all the kids she smuggled out and kept it in a glass jar, buried under a tree in her backyard. After the war, she tried to locate any parents that may have survived it and reunited families. Most had been gassed. Those kids she helped got placed into foster homes or adopted. She was a candidate for the Nobel Peace Prize in 2007.

Which of the seven principles are demonstrated in this story? Explain.

APPENDIX
2

The Crocheted Tablecloth

The brand-new pastor and his wife, newly assigned to their first ministry – to reopen a church in suburban Brooklyn – arrived in early October excited about their opportunities. When they saw their church, it was very run down and needed much work. They set a goal to have everything done in time to have their first service on Christmas Eve.

They worked hard, repairing pews, plastering walls, painting, etc., and on December 18 were ahead of schedule and just about finished.

On December 19, a terrible tempest – a driving rainstorm – hit the area and lasted for two days.

On December 21, the pastor went over to the church. His heart sank when he saw that the roof had leaked, causing a large area of plaster, about 20 feet by 8 feet, to fall off the front wall of the sanctuary just behind the pulpit, beginning about head high.

The pastor cleaned up the mess on the floor, and not knowing what else to do but postpone the Christmas Eve service, headed home. On the way, he noticed a local business that was having a flea market–type sale for charity, so he stopped in. One of the items was a beautiful, handmade, ivory-colored, crocheted tablecloth with exquisite work, fine colors, and a Cross embroidered right in the center. It was just the right size to cover up the hole in the front wall. He bought it and headed back to the church.

By this time it had started to snow. An older woman running from the opposite direction was trying to catch the bus. She missed it. The pastor invited her to wait in the warm church for the next bus, due to arrive 45 minutes later.

She sat in a pew and paid no attention to the pastor while he got a ladder, hangers, etc., to put up the tablecloth as a wall tapestry. The pastor could hardly believe how beautiful it looked, and it covered the entire problem area.

Then he noticed the woman walking down the center aisle. Her face was like a sheet. "Pastor," she asked, "where did you get that tablecloth?"

The pastor explained. The woman asked him to check the lower right corner to see if the initials "EBG" were crocheted into it. They were. These were her initials! She had made this tablecloth 35 years before, in Austria.

The woman could hardly believe it as the pastor told how he had just purchased the tablecloth. The woman explained that before the war she and her husband were well-to-do people in Austria. When the Nazis came, she was forced to leave. Her husband was going to follow her the next week. He was captured, sent to prison. She never saw her husband or her home again.

The pastor wanted to give her the tablecloth, but she insisted the pastor keep it for the church. In return, the pastor offered to drive her home, which was on the other side of Staten Island (she had come to Brooklyn for the day to do housecleaning).

What a wonderful service they had on Christmas Eve. The church was almost full. The music and the spirit were great. At the end of the service, the pastor and his wife greeted everyone at the door, and many said that they would return. One older man, whom the pastor recognized from the neighborhood, continued to sit in one of the pews and stare. The pastor wondered why he wasn't leaving.

The man asked him where he got the tablecloth on the front wall because it was identical to the one that his wife had made years ago when they lived in Austria before the war. He could not understand how there could be two tablecloths so much alike.

He told the pastor how the Nazis came, how he forced his wife to flee for her life. He was supposed to follow her, but he was arrested and put in a prison. He never saw his wife or his home again for all the 35 years in between.

The pastor asked him if he would allow him to take him for a little ride. They drove to Staten Island, to the same address where the pastor had taken the woman three days before.

He helped the man climb three flights of stairs to the woman's apartment and knocked on the door. The pastor saw the greatest Christmas reunion he could ever have imagined.

This true story was told by Pastor Rob Reid.

God's Plan is perfect. Expect the best – demand nothing.

What other principles can you apply to this story? Explain.

Reference Materials

A Book of Wonders and *Psalms for Zero Gravity* by Edward Hays
After Brain Injury: Telling Your Story by Barbara Stahura
The Awakening Universe by Neal Rogin (DVD)
Creation Spirituality and *Whee, We, Wee, All the Way Home* by
    Matthew Fox, OP
Electro-acupressure by Star Tech Health: www.startechhealth.com
Eternal Now (And How to Be There) by Richard Rohr, OFM and
    Thomas Keeting, OCSO (CD)
Healing Relationships, by Fr. Justin Belitz, OFM (CD)
Heterosexual-homosexual continuum – Google: "Kinsey
    continuum"
Homosexuality: *The Test Case for Christian Social Ethics* by
    James P. Hanigan
Ho'oponopono - *The Attractor Factor* and *The Zero Factor* by
    Joe Vitale
Ho'oponopono (CD) by Justin Belitz, OFM
The Invitation by Oriah Mountain Dreamer
The Journey of Man featuring Dr. Spencer Wells, and produced
    by PBS
Louder Than Words: A Mother's Journey in Healing Autism by
    Jenny McCarthy
Man's Judgment of Death and *Twenty Thousand Years in Sing
    Sing* by Lewis Lawes
New Ways Ministries: newwaysministry.org
No Arms, No Legs, No Worries and *Life Without Limbs to Life
    Without Limits* by Nick Vujicic
The Power of Now by Eckhart Tolle
The Power of the Universe (CDs) by Brian Swimme
Prayers for a Planetary Pilgrim by Ed Hays
Sex, Lies and Gender by National Geographic Society (DVD)
Success: Full Living by Justin Belitz, OFM
Success: Full Thinking by Justin Belitz, OFM
Vipassana Meditation: spiritualityandpractice.com
Wellness Pro (Rife machine): Contact Evelyn Easson at
    easson@wico.net or (765) 592- 2192

The Hermitage Catalogue

Compact Disc

QTY	OPUS	TITLE	USA PRICE	AUS PRICE
	OPUS I	**Vol. 1 - A Universal Morning &Evening Meditation** - A set of two meditations; one for morning and one for evening. The image of light is used to represent God and it is specifically created for people of any faith **Vol. 7 - Basic Relaxation** - This CD is specifically designed for people who are beginning meditation or who have trouble relaxing.	$15.00	$30.00
	OPUS II	**Vol. 2 - A Christian Morning & Evening Meditation:** A set of two meditations; one for morning and another for evening. The image of Jesus is used in this CD so that it can be used by any Christian. **Vol. 3 - Contemplative Prayer** -A set of two meditations; one for morning and another for evening. It is an example of passive meditation that can be used by persons of any faith.	$15.00	$30.00
	OPUS III	**Vol. 4 - Creating & Maintaining Ideal Weight:** This CD is designed to help anyone reach ideal weight. **Vol. 16 - Controlling the Smoking Habit - by Therese Coddington** A meditation for those wishing to be non-smokers.	$15.00	$30.00
	OPUS IV	**Vol. 5 - Healing Relationships** - This CD will assist the meditator in developing a positive attitude toward anyone, especially people who are difficult to be with or to work with. One track is designed to guide a single person and the other is designed for a group. **Vol. 10 - Positive Self-Image** - The purpose of this CD is to help the meditator improve self-image. One track explains the process of how mind and brain create self-image. Another track has a meditation based on several positive affirmations designed to improve anyone's self image.	$15.00	$30.00

	OPUS V	**Vol. 6 - Healing Self** - A meditation for anyone who is ill, either physically, mentally, emotionally, psychologically, or spiritually. **Vol. 9 - Healing Others** -This CD is designed for family and/or friends of a patient. It is a companion to Vol. 6	$15.00	$30.00
	OPUS VI	**Vol. 8 - The Lords Prayer and the Prayer of St. Francis** - The meditations on this CD are examples of how a person can use meditation on any given text. **Vol. 14 - Peace** -This meditation is designed to help the meditator develop a cosmic dimension of peace. Track 3 is for an individual and Track 4 is for a group.	$15.00	$30.00
	OPUS VII	**Vol. 13 - Children's Meditation - by Daniel McRoberts** This CD is especially designed for children, but can also be used by adults. Track 1 is for meditation and Track 2 is to assist the meditator achieve sleep. The voice is a 13 year old boy. **Vol. 18 Angels Among Us.** Track 3 of this unique recording offers an explanation of angels as God's messengers. Track 4 offers a guided meditation to help you connect with your "angels" when working through challenges, difficulties or planning your future.	$15.00	$30.00
	OPUS VIII	**Vol. 11 - My Friend the Sea** -Poetry is meditation! This recording has selections that reflect on some beautiful moments in the life of Fr. Justin. It is hoped that your listening will motivate you to write your own poetry. **Vol. 12 - The 23rd Psalm & St. Francis Canticle of Praise** -This recording contains two examples of how meditation can be used with any familiar text, scripture, poem, or prayer.	$15.00	$30.00
	OPUS IX	**Vol. 15 - Music for Meditation - Flutist: Sr. Barbara Piller, OSF / Harpist: Mary Wild** A recording of music appropriate for meditation. Track 1 is flute only and Track 2 is harp only. **Vol. 17- Music for Meditation - Clarinet: Rob Carroll / Synthesizer: Andy Consentino** A recording of music appropriate for meditation. Track 1 is clarinet only and Track 2 is synthesizer only.	$15.00	$30.00

	OPUS X	**Vol. 19 - Learning (made fast and easy) for students only** - This CD is specifically for students, to show them how to use meditation to learn faster and easier. It contains other suggestions for effective study as well. **Vol. 20 - Teaching (made efficient and effective) for teachers only** - This CD is for teachers who wish to be more efficient and effective in the classroom. It deals specifically with relaxation, visualization and other tools to enhance learning.	$15.00	$30.00
	OPUS XI	**Meditation: Ho'oponopono (and other contemplative meditations) – by Fr. Justin Belitz, OFM, Music by John Cannaday, Vocalist: Tim Jeffers** Track 1: Ho'oponopono (explanation) Track 2: Ho'oponopono (experience) Track 3: Be Life, Share Life Track 4: Spirit of the Living God	$15.00	$30.00

Albums and Books

	Title	USA PRICE	AUS PRICE
	Success: Full Living (Album): "A Mini-Retreat on 3 CDs" by Fr. Justin Belitz, OFM"	$30.00	$75.00
	Success: Full *Living* (Book): "A Contemporary Approach to Responsible Spirituality" by Fr. Justin Belitz, OFM	$15.00	$20.00
	Success: Full *Thinking* (Book): "Tapping into the Unlimited Resources of Mind" – by Fr. Justin Belitz, OFM	$15.00	$20.00
	Success: Full *Relating* (Book): "Spirituality for the 21st century and beyond" by Fr. Justin Belitz, OFM	$15.00	$20.00

QTY	SIZE	**Wear White on Wednesdays for Peace**
	LARGE	In November of 2007, Fr. Justin presented a workshop in Australia titled: You Can Make a Difference. Scott Shelley, a participant in this workshop, decided to start a worldwide movement for peace. His card reads: "Wherever you're going or what ever you are doing, you are invited to wear white every Wednesday for world peace." The Hermitage is supporting this effort by providing T-Shirts with this message on the back: Wear White Every Wednesday for World Peace". On the front of the T-Shirt is the logo of the Hermitage and a picture of the Dove of Peace. The T-Shirts come in size large and extra-large. The Cost of the T-Shirt is $15.00, shipping and handling is $3.00 Please help us bring peace to this planet !!!!
	X LARGE	

Order online at www.FrJustin-Hermitage.org or copy and/or fill out this form and include credit card info, check or money order made out to:

U.S. Order Form

Order on line at
www.FrJustin-Hermitage.org
or fill out this form and include credit card info,
check or money order made out to:
"Franciscan Hermitage"
3650 E 46th Street
Indianapolis, IN 46205
or Call Monday – Friday 12:00-5:00 pm EST
(317) 545-0742
e-mail: frjustin@frjustin-hermitage.org
websites: www.FrJustin-Hermitage.org

	QTY	AMT
Compact Discs @ $15.00 each		
Success: Full Living Album @ $30.00 each		
Books @ $15.00 each		
T-Shirt(s) @ 15.00 each L XL		
Donation		
Shipping & Handling - $2 for 1st item ($1 for each additional)		
Total:		

Name: _____

Address: _____

City:_____State:_____Zip:_____

Phone: (Day)_____ (Evening)_____

Check: Y__N__Number_____

VISA ⬤⬤ ▭▭ _____

Exp Date:_____/_____

Signature: _____

Australian Order Form

Fill out this form and include credit card info,
check or money order made out to:

PEACE BE STILL
Lot 100 Chittering Road
Lower Chittering WA 6084
Phone: 0II-61-8-9571-8108
peacebestill@iinet.net.au

		QTY	AMT
Compact Discs @ $30.00 each			
Success: Full Living Album @ $75.00 each			
Books @ $20.00 each			
T-Shirt(s) @ 15.00 each L XL			
Donation			
Postage & Handling (Within Australia) Folder Set – Success: Full Living Album $12.00 per set Individual CD & DVD $5.00 per unit			
Total:			

LaVergne, TN USA
05 August 2010
192220LV00003B/2/P